ONE
LAST
DROP

ONE LAST DROP

The Ripple Effect of Alcohol, Athletics, and Love

RYAN STOCK

One Last Drop

First Edition 2021

ISBN: 978-1-7368587-0-7

CONSCIOUS
HUMAN

Find Your Path, Start Your Journey

This book is just the beginning. While *One Last Drop* is your introduction to the world of athletics, love, and establishing new and healthy habits in your life, there's a lot more we still have to unpack. Be sure to visit ***consciousryan.com*** for more information, resources, and guidance on how Ryan will help with your journey in life after One Last Drop.

Once you join our One Drop reader community you will explore different areas of your life taking your game, and life, to a higher and healthier level. Our One Last Drop and Conscious Athlete communities allow you to find balance again in life, love, and your athletic career. Find your unhealthy habits, your unconscious limiting beliefs, then let's make lasting, positive changes.

Please join me at ***consciousryan.com*** to get access to exercises and tools mentioned in this book and learn how you can:

1. **Visit Consciousryan.com** - One Last Drop is a great start, you're already on the right path. But if you have more questions, or want to join a more conscious movement in sports or outside of sports, you'll find everything you need there. You can also find the Conscious Athlete Guide and app to help you reframe your negative thoughts around sports, your life, and your relationships. The Conscious Athlete Guide will compliment this book in helping you clear and calm your mind and, in turn, take your game and life to a higher level.

2. **Download the Conscious Athlete app** - Download the app for meditations and other powerful mindfulness and movement exercises. You can watch Ryan lead guided meditations on a variety

of topics, see him working with other professional athletes sharing their experiences, both positive and negative, and witness how they use Ryan's program to become more balanced.

3. **VIP and Team Opportunities** - Do you want the most intimate and impactful experiences for your life, or your team? Visit consciousryan.com to learn more on how to schedule a 30-minute discovery call to work with Ryan one-on-one, or to learn how he can help your team or organization.

Ready to schedule a call? Visit *consciousryan.com/coaching* to speak directly with me, and begin the most impactful and life-changing experience he offers.

Foreword

"Isn't it marvelous to discover that you're the one you've been waiting for? That you are your own freedom?" ~Byron Katie

When was the last time you found true freedom? From something that was keeping you stuck. Alcohol. Cigarettes. Sugar. A relationship. A job. Anything. Did you wait for something outside you to change? Or did you look within?

Ryan Stock has found freedom within, and not just from alcohol. Through his journey to stop drinking, he has created a fully free human experience for himself. Mind. Body. Spirit. His self-exploration is not only admirable, but it is powerful beyond measure. And, it's because he stopped waiting for someone or something other than himself.

Every month, I receive thousands of letters and emails from people who have found freedom from alcohol with This Naked Mind. But, I rarely get to meet any of them in person - that's just the nature of being an author with a ton of online content and an app and more than 350,000 people who have gone through The Alcohol Experiment.

One of those emails came in early 2021 from Ryan. I was honored when he asked if he could interview me for his documentary film, One Last Drop. It was an incredible privilege to meet him and his crew in person late that summer when they drove across the country to spend a day with me.

Beyond the interviews I do for This Naked Mind podcast, I really don't have the opportunity to see and experience people in real life, to actually sit down with them and dig into all the things that are so important to them. The time I spent with Ryan was a true gift.

Ryan breathes from a place of truth and generosity. He embraces every single part of his journey. He recognizes two things: We can be both a masterpiece and a work in progress at the same time and that type of existence is essential for continued growth. We all fall. The power is in getting back up.

The time I spent with Ryan was insightful, enlightening, and so very therapeutic. So many highlights from our conversations continue to resonate with me …

Learning about how he is driven at soul level by his love for his son. As a parent myself, I feel this so deeply.

Witnessing his dedication to yoga and his physical health - how his conscious connection to his mind, body, and soul keep him constantly in touch with how he wants to feel and show up in this world.

Feeling his passion for making a difference in people's lives. Using our knowledge to create a ripple effect – a power into which others can step when they are ready – is one of our most precious gifts as humans.

Crying in solidarity with Ryan as we talked about our vulnerabilities.

At the end of the day, I think the reason I appreciate Ryan's magnificent power so greatly is because he embodies so much of what I have identified as essential values for myself and those I invite into my circle. We are masters of our own energy and we use it to set new standards. We refuse to stay stuck waiting for a safe feeling to propel us forward. We stay grounded in curiosity, not judgment. And, we take care of ourselves first, so we can show up as the best versions of ourselves for everyone around us.

This is where we start. And this is what keeps us moving forward.

"Love starts within. Enjoy the journey." @ConsciousRyan on
Instagram on February 13, 2022
~Annie Grace

Table of Content

Preface

A dichotomy: a clear distinction between two things.

A word we don't use (at least I don't) or hear that often. Yet it's the word that became the overarching theme of not only this book but also my life of late.

I was in love with a girl. I was genuinely in love with her and wanted the best for her, but I was a shitty partner. I thought that I needed to have control over the relationship, and to some degree my partner, in order to be the best partner I could be. I see now how unhealthy that viewpoint is in a relationship.

The same was true of my relationship with sports. I wanted to be the best at everything I did, especially with my illustrious athletic playing career and then my coaching career that soon followed. Failure was not an option—it was unacceptable.

How can you be mindful and not attached to results when either you win or lose, succeed or fail?

Mindfulness and meditation are intended to help with the ongoing battle of conquering desires or cravings. They exist to help overcome aversions or dislikes too. When we are truly mindful, we are focused on that moment, that play, and that breath.

So how the hell can one be mindful and be the best? How can you want to dominate your competition and feel compassion for them at the same time?

There was a spiritual dichotomy too. I believe in a higher power—a reason for us to do right, to live right, and to treat people right. Most people take that to mean they need religion in their life, a structure to their faith. I do not.

How and why would a higher power focus on which religion is right or wrong? Wouldn't it focus on love, kindness, and empathy? Wouldn't it focus on treating people with respect and acknowledging differences while being inclusive? Wouldn't a supreme being be more focused on these elements of our existence?

Finally, with my world of mindfulness, meditation, and yoga, I was trying as best as I could to be present with my emotions and thoughts. I also wanted to be at peace with other areas personally and professionally.

This line of thinking means that, for the most part, you should not rely heavily on intoxicants of any kind, especially to the point where you are numb or no longer feeling or thinking clearly.

You should not, in theory, be drinking or smoking to not feel. You should not be trying to escape from emotions, failures, relationships, success or the lack of in a business.

And while I was drinking less in quantity for the past several years, I was drinking more often so as not to feel. My drinking had become heavy and unhealthy.

So heavy, in fact, that my life was jeopardized.

The heavy drinking led to a bottoming out. Finally, I realized that something had to change when an ultimatum was set initially by one person.

I don't say that lightly; something had to change or I'd die.

The mindfulness and meditation business I started was beginning to flounder. The girl that I loved decided she could no longer be with me. My life was falling apart at the seams as they say in the sports world.

For me, giving up drinking and writing this book was my way out. It was therapeutic—a way to stop the madness that had consumed me.

This book, as a result, is intensely personal.

I have used fake names in a few places but the stories are real—all my deepest darkest secrets are out there. This includes my recovery from alcohol, what it did to those around me, and how it fucked up the relationship with the girl I genuinely thought was the love of my life.

It also describes how I skated by for years on being a great athlete, possessing charm, good looks, a nice smile, and a high level of intelligence. All of this even though I was by most counts close to or already dependent on alcohol.

I was a living dichotomy. I was a mindful drunk.

That shit is tough to write; it's even tougher to share with the world. But like the dichotomy, what I've learned is that two seemingly conflicting things can be true at the same time about the same thing.

You can believe in God and not have a religion. You can be trying as hard as you can in a relationship and be a shitty partner. Two people can be madly in love and want a relationship to work but it doesn't—it won't.

You can make a heartfelt attempt to connect with someone, to help a relationship, and it works perfectly. You feel amazing, and so do they.

You can make a similar attempt later in the same relationship or a different relationship, and this time you make it worse. The ripple effects of that effort send the relationship into a tailspin that never recovers. All this from what was a heartfelt attempt to make things better.

There are all kinds of examples of this in life. At times, we are trying to help but hurting. Our awareness and communication levels are unable to provide us the result we desire.

The same is true of this book. What will be beneficial for many may seem dangerous to others.

It's also important to mention here that my path to recovery was different from most people's experience, what most people need. I did many things you aren't supposed to do according to the truest form of an AA program, for instance. As for those that would consider themselves to have a problem with alcohol, or the socially feared term of being labeled an alcoholic.

On my path, I didn't go to rehab. I talked to my ex-partner much sooner than anyone would suggest. I read other books that most in the recovery world would frown upon. I didn't dive head in and blindly accept everything, surrender to everything like most people in recovery are told to do.

That doesn't mean it was right or wrong for anyone else; it was just right for me.

If you are picking up this book because you may have a problem, don't get caught up in labels like an alcoholic or addict. This isn't that kind of book.

Read it, take in my experiences and my lessons learned, and then start to explore some of the habits that you have in your life. It will help immensely in that regard—in spotting your bad habits, helping you feel like you're not alone with them, and in taking steps in the right direction.

Some of my experiences like the time I bottomed out emotionally, which you will read about next, are jarring. They're graphic in detail.

This book isn't to compare war stories. It's not to brag about my failures or accomplishments. This book is to tell real, raw, and authentic stories about a struggle with alcohol that centered around not wanting to feel, not wanting to be alone with my thoughts, and not wanting to experience life in the way it was meant to be experienced. Take a moment, take a breath, and think deeper into the message behind the introduction below. Then when you are ready, begin your journey with me, with my recovery starting with my emotional bottoming out.

Introduction

Welcome to the hardest, and most rewarding, project I've ever undertaken. That's saying a lot too. You'll understand why as you read.

The project? It's an emotional, vulnerable, thought-provoking, and Forrest Gump-like tale of the first 30 days of my recovery from heavy dependence on alcohol.

Dependency was not in the form most associated with alcohol, drugs, or anything for that matter habit-wise. I never shook without alcohol; I never had physical withdrawals. I drank way less in the end than when I did at my peak of alcohol consumption.

The difference in the end was I was drinking to avoid emotions, celebrate success, or because I was sad. I could always find a reason to drink or an excuse I should say. I had gone from drinking in excess to drinking to become numb.

I thought alcohol was a friend of mine. I thought it made me funnier, more confident, and better in bed among many other things. None of those things is true.

It all came crashing down one day, and I started writing to help process it all.

In daily letters to my son, I weave in and out of the past and the present blending the experiences of my life—experiences that centered around alcohol, athletics, and love. Reflecting on how the combination of those three things made for a dangerous cocktail (see what I did there) in my adult life that resulted in a bottoming out that started on day one of this very book.

My hope is that Owen, my son, will learn from my mistakes, understand and enjoy more of the positives of his life, and that you (the reader) will benefit from accompanying us on that journey.

There are two big revelations upon finishing the book: first, being alone with your thoughts sucks. It's scary in that space when you're alone with just your thoughts. Many of us fill that space with distraction.

That space between distractions, our first and our next, becomes intimidating. It becomes so intimidating that it leads to mind-numbing habits like the abuse of alcohol, drugs, sex, gambling, social media, video games, and even food.

The vice that fills that space differs for each individual.

That leads to the second revelation. Distractions lead to habits, which become a slippery slope toward addiction that even the strongest mind and body find difficult to escape.

And while there are several forms of addictions or ways to numb the mind, some are more dangerous than others.

Certain habits are more socially acceptable than others are too. Drinking, for example, is not only socially acceptable but also encouraged. However, some people have a drink, then another one, and then another. It starts to become an issue.

Some check their phones, get another notification moments later, and check their phone again. You can't have a conversation without them checking their phone. It's annoying. This pattern repeats until social media and their phone controls their lives. It's their dopamine hit; it's how they feel alive.

Others feel full from their meal but want to eat one more chocolate, have more cake and ice cream, or eat another serving of their meal knowing they are no longer hungry.

Some numb their minds with video games, or weed, or both.

All these are layers to what at first seems like a normal habit with one common purpose in mind: not to feel at our most vulnerable levels and not to be alone with our thoughts.

What we don't realize in this slow decline, our mind-numbing descent, is that it starts to affect everything in our lives. Our relationships become less healthy for us and our partners. Our job performance suffers even if we don't think it's the case at the moment.

Your health, your happiness all slowly decline until this habit is no longer providing you any joy. It's just getting you back to a place where you can function. The habit starts to become the way you make it through the day. You're addicted.

The purpose of this book is to show you exactly what I was thinking. You get my thoughts, my feelings, my experiences in my life leading up to the danger zone of needing recovery and the days in and around that recovery.

I let you, the reader, into my mind—an advanced meditative mind that had worked for years on quieting itself, on being comfortable in a vulnerable space, on being comfortable being alone with my thoughts.

Then you witness my realization that it wasn't enough; none of it was. Alcohol won.

True balance is not attainable in life. People misunderstand that. When we hear the term the "right path," we usually think that means the correct path. That's not how the original teaching was intended. The right path was meant along the lines of righting a ship.

We go through life making a series of corrections in our personal lives, in love, and even in our athletic careers or professions. Those corrections keep us balanced.

After reading my book, you'll be better equipped to spot your unhealthy habits, when they're growing, and when it's time to step away from them. When you need to right your own ship.

That won't be easy—growth, meaningful change, never is. It's painful.

Ultimately, it will lead you to a healthier, more enjoyable, and more mindful life. A life where you are good with being exposed, raw, and vulnerable; a life where you'll be better equipped to handle difficult times.

But more importantly, it exposes a life where you enjoy the positive experiences at a new level, a deeper level. Isn't that what we are all looking for—to feel more intensely, to love more deeply, and to feel more alive?

It's scary. I know. It's intimidating. But there's a reason you picked up this book. Sometimes we need to go on a journey of change, of growth, and of discovery.

That journey starts right here, right now for me. I hope it does for you too.

In darkness and in light,

Ryan

680 DAYS BEFORE DAY 1

Hazard Lights

"EVERYBODY FIGHTS DEMONS. SOME ARE WORSE THAN OTHERS."
— JOHN DALY, GOLFER

September 30, 2018, I think. I could find the actual date if I wanted to, but I don't. This is a couple weeks before I'd be officially divorced. I do know that date, October 29, 2018.

On this particular day, a Sunday, the Chiefs were playing. My Sunday routine when I didn't have my son usually consisted of going to a bar to watch football and drink beer. Then go home with some more alcohol, watch the Sunday night football game, and then pass out early.

I was always too smart to drive too drunk, to get too fucked up. That's how I got away with things for so long. I was great at towing the line and driving cautiously when I had been drinking.

This day was different though. Laura, Owen's mother and my ex-wife, had asked me earlier that week if I had ever thought about killing myself to make it easier on Owen and her. I knew she didn't mean that. She was being shitty to try and hurt me. Toward the end she did this a lot. She would say the most hurtful things to me to get a reaction. I know now that was her way of getting me to show I still cared. At this point, in our relationship, it didn't get a reaction from me. I was tired of fighting. I didn't care. But it still really hurt. It was still really heavy for me to hold

5

that space. That the mother of my child would say some shit like that just to hurt me even if she did not mean it is fucked up.

After leaving the bar, I decided to drive to a strip club down the road. Almost halfway between the bar and my house, I thought I could still make it home. Bad idea.

A couple hours later, several drinks later, I was good and fucked up. I didn't want to die, but you get to a space when you are bottoming out that you really don't care if you live. The alcohol, the pain, the divorce, and the failures going on in my life—it was too much. I drove home thinking I was still good to drive. You do that too when you are really drunk. "I can make it home," you think.

On my way home, I was sober enough to remember everything but way too drunk to be driving. I was turning left onto a street that had four lanes on one side and two lanes on the other side of the median—six lanes total with a curb in between them. But it was late at night now on a Sunday night. There was no traffic, a ghost town of sorts on the road.

The street now looked to me like it was four lanes without a median. What you see normally in most smaller towns, which is where I am from originally. Four lanes, two for each side, with no median. So I turned left into what I thought was the far-right lane of the way I was supposed to be headed. It was instead the far-left lane, the turning left lane, of what was normally oncoming traffic.

No one was in any of the lanes, thank God. No one was even out at this point. I even caught what was happening right as I was about to enter the oncoming traffic lanes and swerved to the other side of the median where I was supposed to be headed. Being that drunk though, I caught it a split second too late. Both left tires clipped the curb. Both left tires went flat.

Again, by the grace of whatever God or higher power you believe in, about 500 feet away was a gas station. About 1,000 feet from there, within walking distance, was a hotel. I somehow navigated my car to the gas station, parked it, and then stumbled around trying to figure out what the hell I was going to do for the night.

After I parked, I walked next door and got a hotel room. I left my phone on the ice machine right in front of my car. Yes, I left my cell phone on an ice machine sometime around midnight at a 7/11. But I was good to drive, I thought.

I had to use the Find My iPhone app in the morning to find it. That took about 45 minutes. Turns out, I was not good to drive, not even close.

When I woke up that morning at around 8 a.m., the end of the evening was a blur. I remember most of it, but parts of it I don't. I was at the gas station the next day, and I remember vividly thinking, "What the fuck am I going to do? Where do I even start?"

I couldn't drive anywhere. Money wasn't necessarily an issue, but was I going to have to get a tow truck? Would someone bring the tires to me? What was going to happen to the rest of my day?

Keep in mind I'm in linen khaki pants and a Chiefs T-shirt from the night before. I had showered and smelled nice and clean but my mind and soul felt dirty.

Most people that saw me early the next morning had assumed I just hit the curb that morning on my way to work or something. I didn't correct them.

Here's where things started to look up. And I'll admit it, to this day I don't know what I would have done without this crazy shit happening.

I'm standing outside my car, just standing there looking at two flat tires with no idea what to do. I had clothes on from the night before, and I was trying to act like I have my shit together. Well, more like trying to hold my shit together. I'm in a pretty bad space at this point.

Right then, (I'm not exaggerating) right at that moment, a car pulls up in the spot next to mine. It was an old beat-up car, like a Trans-Am or something, from the late '90s or maybe early 2000s. It was around 20 or so years old, but it ran; it ran pretty well actually.

That's because the guy in it was a mechanic. His job was to go around the city and help repair people's cars. That was his actual job—show up to a site, fix the car, and leave.

He was in between jobs at this moment and parked in the spot right next to mine. He had just stopped to get a drink before he picked up another call. Think about the odds of that happening. This big ass city and the exact nonjudgmental person that I need to pull up in the spot right next to mine at that exact moment does just that.

He made some small talk with me. I don't even remember his name, but he asked if I needed help. I said, "Yeah that would be great, but I have no idea where to start."

He proceeded to take the next three or so hours out of his day to help me get my life back together. We started by going to get one new tire, so we could put that on the car with my spare tire. It took us three tire shops to find one that had the correct size and brand of tire.

We then drove my car back to this specific tire place for them to put on another tire and then balance and align the existing ones. All said and done the damage to the car wasn't that bad. It was more to my mind, my heart, and my soul.

Once everything was repaired, I honestly could not have paid this man enough. I tipped him handsomely and will remember that day for the rest of my life—that dark day.

The reality of the day, this day before it all began, is that we all feel these deep, intense pains at some point in our lives. We can try and do all these things to ignore them, block them off, and be averse to them, but they won't go away.

If we don't answer them, if we don't acknowledge our bad habits, and if we don't do the work on ourselves then those demons will win out. We can't keep feeding that bad wolf as they say.

We should instead choose to acknowledge that side of our lives—to hear it and feel it. But to move on from it quicker is where we leave the space for growth. I see that now; I feel that now.

You can't just block it out; you can't drink it away; you have to tackle these issues head on. Talk about them, shine light into the darkness in an open and vulnerable space, and be real about it.

Find people in your life that are still good with you because those people do exist. We, or at least I, didn't think those people existed before. Or if they did, that they will still love me with all my baggage and all my bullshit. But they do. They will still love you just as they do with me.

And to me that's the most beautiful part of life—the darkness that forces us to surrender, which then forces us to see the true beauty and light within.

Remember, we're not even to Day 1 yet!

176 DAYS BEFORE DAY 1

A Stubborn Learner

Most bottom out physically first. I was no different.

Before we get to Day 1, my emotional date, we need to talk about an experience that would have stopped most. A warning shot that was fired to me, mentally and physically. It wasn't enough. I didn't stop. I wasn't ready.

I chose to keep drinking.

Keep in mind that this traumatic event happened, and I didn't stop drinking. Well, I stopped for around eight weeks. I could always stop for long periods of time like that.

But, inevitably, I'd find a way back to visit my friend, alcohol. I'd find some excuse to drink—something I felt deserved celebrating, or something too frustrating for me to handle on my own. I always found my way back.

The date was February 16, which was the first time I honestly thought, "Oh shit, this is a problem."

Danielle (my partner at the time, someone I loved intensely during the most difficult time of my life, and the person I'll refer to often in these writings) and I had just finished a yoga workshop for Valentine's Day. I

11

drank heavily the night before, had food poisoning a couple weeks before that, and the Chiefs had just won the Super Bowl. (I'm a HUGE Chiefs fan! I celebrated their first Super Bowl by drinking so much that I blacked out.)

All of these heavy drinking nights occurred within a couple weeks of each other. And as you might imagine, this was tough on a heavy drinker for a number of reasons.

For a couple weeks, I hadn't been tasting food, and my appetite had slowly faded. I don't usually condone drinking energy drinks, but I was back on them as I felt my energy levels slipping because I wasn't eating.

I had not seen a doctor about any of this. With an athlete and coaching mindset, I was too tough to ask for help.

Danielle and I went out to eat that night after the workshop. I barely ate again. I had two vodka waters with the meal. We went home and went to bed. I felt relatively normal, a little off, but nothing worth noting.

I woke up around 3 a.m. and went into the guest bathroom as I knew I was going to throw up. I assumed it was food poisoning again.

I usually have an iron stomach but can always tell when I am going to throw up. I was right. I did.

This time it was 100 percent blood. No food just blood. I went back to bed telling Danielle I just threw up blood. Yes, I went right back to bed after essentially projectile vomiting massive amounts of blood. In hindsight, I see how foolish that was.

I threw up again at around 6 a.m. Once again, it was all blood, and the sun was now up. I was going to have my then three-year-old son, Owen, over for the next couple of days. I didn't want to miss spending time with him, so I was going to "tough it out."

Danielle had to go teach yoga at 8 a.m. until around 10 a.m. I was going to be alone with my son until she got back. My son arrived at around 8:30 a.m., and I turned on a kids movie. We cuddled up on an oversized recliner.

It was 9 a.m., and I had to throw up again.

I move to the guest bathroom and throw up blood, again. It's now a little after 9 a.m., and my son is asking if I'm OK as I throw up blood for the third time in a little over seven hours. It's not a little blood either; it's a lot. Every time I throw up, it's a lot of blood.

I remember thinking, "I only have so much of that in me, I suppose."

Once Danielle arrives, I let her know what's going on, and we decide I need to have someone take a look. I go to Urgent Care although I am still not sure if I need help (idiot, I know), and they send me straight to the ER. They don't even look at me.

That's not good.

Meanwhile, Danielle sends my son to his grandma's; he is safe. I can focus on healing. I had no idea how long or difficult that task would be.

What would happen next is that I would spend the next 72 hours in intensive care as a result of a small tear in my throat—a combination of an initial bout of food poisoning that spiraled into drinking more energy drinks, capped off by a couple heavy nights of drinking.

I lost half the blood in my body. I had several pints of blood transfused into my body, and even got some stitches in my eye from a fall I took when I was trying to throw up more blood on my own early on in my hospital stay.

The most eye-opening part, I think, was that I remember lying in bed in intensive care wanting the doctor to tell me to stop drinking or to tell me that I had a problem. He didn't.

They kept asking how much I drank, and I answered honestly: a couple beers every day and sometimes, a shot with them. Occasionally, on the weekends or on special occasions, I'd drink heavily. I'd binge drink.

Tests came back normal. My liver was fine, and, physically, I didn't have a drinking problem. The problem was in my mind.

Losing half the blood in my body, almost dying, still wasn't enough to get me to stop.

Having my three-year-old son watch me throw up blood and ask me if I was OK wasn't enough.

It took another 176 days before I would bottom out. 176 more days before there was enough pain physically, mentally, and emotionally that I would stop drinking. 176 more days before Day 1.

Week 1

Awaken

DAY 1

Two Sides

> "I WAS NEVER ADDICTED TO ONE THING, I WAS ADDICTED TO FILLING A
> VOID WITHIN MYSELF WITH THINGS OTHER THAN MY OWN LOVE."
> — YUNG PUEBLO, AUTHOR

Lesson Learned – Today is the last night I take a drink. I was frustrated that my ex, Danielle, wouldn't see me to further discuss our relationship. My answer to that, as was to most problems at this time, was to buy a pint of Tito's vodka (my alcohol of choice) and chug it in 30 minutes. I write Day 1 of this journal to no one in particular. Incoherent thoughts are really all I have, then I go buy more alcohol. I don't remember how the night ends.

Lowest Low – I wake up at around 3 a.m. in panic not remembering how the night ended. Danielle broke things off with me. She told me she couldn't see me anymore, but this was pretty common between us at this point. We'd been on and off for months.

I wrote to my son, Owen, day 1 of the journal tonight. I had no idea the journal, this book, was beginning.

My heart is racing. There's a glass half full of straight vodka left on a railing right outside my bedroom door. I chug the vodka straight. It's warm, and I can't taste anything. I chase it with a half-full glass of warm fruit punch Gatorade.

I stare at the ceiling, awake in bed, for the next four hours. Tonight has to be the last night I drink. Everything has collapsed around me. I've bottomed out emotionally.

15

Owen,

Your dad has a confession to make. For the last year, maybe two, I've been living a double life. On the surface, I'm a calm and collected meditator, a former star athlete, a successful NCAA basketball coach, and a successful mental trainer and yoga instructor to pro and college athletes all across the world.

I rarely raise my voice. I don't go out much or do drugs. I've never been in any legal trouble. In the community, I'm well liked by most. The only conflicts I have are if a person is too negative or has a bad energy. I don't like to be around those types of people. I don't like people that talk shit about others or want to see others fail.

As a result of these things, I keep a tight circle of friends and family. I like it that way. I'm guarded emotionally.

Below the surface, I have a dark side, a bad wolf—one that I've fed with alcohol since the age of 18. That wolf has become too powerful for me now. It's too strong. I can no longer control it.

I have no choice but to surrender to it, to starve that control that the substance has over me. I'm ready to ask for help and to start a recovery process that is one of the most intimidating things I have ever done in my life.

Alcoholism, addiction runs in our family. I'm not sure to what degree it has its hands on me yet. I do know that my life has become unbearable and that aside from you I don't have a lot going for me personally, professionally, or emotionally.

Something has to change, and that change starts tonight. Well, in the morning, I decided to tie one last drunken night on as you aren't with me tonight. I'll see you tomorrow afternoon. I have some things to sort out before then mentally, physically, and emotionally.

I'm writing these letters to you while you are close to the age I was when it became noticeable that I was going to be an above average athlete. That athletic ability led to a free college education and then a professional career that would takeoff and wind down a path that ultimately led me here.

While I don't blame athletics, or the success I had in athletics, on how things ended up, it certainly played a part. Some of my fondest memories were created as a young athlete and some of the funniest too.

What I'd like to do for you is blend past athletic memories with what's happening each day in my recovery—perhaps a lesson learned or a memory triggered.

The first athletic memory that comes to mind was when I was around five years old. I was playing soccer much like you play right now. You actually started a couple years before me. Your first game was at the age of two.

On my team, I was one of the few kids that could score. I didn't chase the ball around like so many kids do at that age.

I was also athletic enough that I could score multiple goals in one game. I remember scoring as many as four later in my youth career.

The funny story I want to share with you today, because I need to, has to do with my first time being a team captain.

Keep in mind that I was all of five years old and not exactly a rock of emotional stability at this point in my life. Hell, I'm not exactly a rock of emotional stability at THIS point in my life either. But I digress back to five-year-old me.

I trot out for the coin toss, the first one I have ever taken part in, and I get the responsibility of calling the coin flip.

A lot of pressure for a five-year-old, or so I thought. What I call I don't remember, but the fact that I called it wrong I certainly do. I started crying like a baby thinking I cost our team the game by losing the coin flip.

All that happens with the loss of the coin flip, for those that don't know, is you either get the ball in the first half or the second half. It makes no difference in the result of the game. It makes even less of a difference at the age of five.

It was effective foreshadowing, however, of the competitiveness I would possess and how much I hated losing in life no matter what the game or competition would be.

DAY 2

A Giant Problem

Lesson Learned — I called Nikki, my sister and Owen's aunt who's been in recovery for 16 years, first thing this morning and figured out what I need to do—or more realistically, where to begin.

I tried to call my former girlfriend, Danielle, at work.

I leave a really emotional voicemail. Terrible idea. I'm a wreck.

Lowest Low — I've been through some shit. I've seen and experienced some terrible things. Today may have been the most challenging of them all. To make that first phone call asking others for help, to admit your weaknesses and your failures—it's incredibly difficult.

It takes every ounce of mental and physical energy I have to simply stay calm. And this is coming from someone who teaches yoga and meditates every day. I'm guessing this will get easier. Damn, I hope so.

Owen,

If I have felt like this before, I can't remember it—this feeling of helplessness, heartbreak, failure, and of being an imposter in so many ways.

I was trying my best, the best my current awareness allowed. My best as a partner, as a professional, and as a father. I think I succeeded in only one, but that was the most important one—caring for you, loving you, and being a good father for you.

I think that may also be the hardest part of all of this for me right now—knowing that I was trying to be a good person, a good partner, a successful entrepreneur, and, most importantly, an incredible father.

I've done one of those things consistently the past several months.

After another conversation last night with Danielle, my partner this past year, I saw I've hurt her and been manipulative in a number of ways even when I was trying to be a good partner, at least I thought I was trying.

Speaking of love, one of my favorite tracks by philosopher Alan Watts talks about surrendering to love—how powerless that can feel and how scary that can be for a person. At first, I tell Danielle I'm ready to do that for her, but after more reflection, more deep thought I realize I don't need to surrender to a love for her.

I need to surrender to a love for me. I need to love myself, to believe in myself.

After all, why would I choose to drink like I have been if ultimately I didn't have that love for myself? That's deep but true. I don't love myself, and until I do, none of this other shit will matter.

I can't be the father, the professional I need to be until I love me. It's strange how that works, yet at the same time how could that not be the case? In love, we always want the other person to make us happy (if I can only find the right girl, I will be happy.) I see now that's not the case.

My to-do list today was all about cleaning up the pieces of my life. A journey that will take months not hours. What used to be a daily to-do list now feels like it will take a lifetime.

Stay sober today, meditate, help others, repeat. I'm guessing that's where that 'one day at a time' mantra will come into play?

I reached out to everyone in and around my professional life letting them know I'd be stepping back from things for a little while, moving slower on my end. Everyone was really receptive, really positive.

19

My friend, Anthony, who runs the yoga studio where I teach had some really kind and encouraging words. Wes, the leader of the accelerator company that helps me out professionally, was really positive in letting me know what he thought of me and my potential once I got healthy again. That felt reassuring.

The hardest part for me has been how I made Danielle feel and what the future holds for us. I think I've known for a while I need help (maybe unconsciously, if that makes sense.)

It probably doesn't. I'm still cloudy with all of this—my mind cluttered, raw, and exposed.

You can't even read yet, but writing to you has really helped me during these times. I just needed to get all these thoughts out because my alarm was set for 6 a.m., and it's 6 a.m. now. I didn't sleep but was instead staring at the ceiling again.

I can't remember a conversation that was as difficult or emotional for me in my life as the one I had with Danielle today. Luckily, I was able to pick you up soon after, around 3 p.m., and you instantly make my life brighter. I feel lighter, and I breathe easier. Your love and touch makes me feel happy and joyful inside.

I'm lucky to have you in my life. I'm grateful.

I needed help, and I see that now. That journey continues today no matter how intimidating that may be for me.

I'm reminded of another time I was greatly intimidated in my life— my athletic life. I felt helpless and powerless even scared of what might happen.

I couldn't have been more than six years old but could already score multiple baskets on a ten-foot regulation basketball goal. It wasn't uncommon in our basketball games for our team to win by a score of 12–4 with me scoring 10 of our 12 points.

Where then, you ask, did this crippling intimidation come from? What could be so bad for someone that was still so young? Well, I checked out the team schedule on our refrigerator at home and saw that we were playing the Giants.

I, naturally, assumed they were really going to be actual giants. I refused to go.

My parents tried to reason with me pleading that they weren't REALLY giants, but I knew they were lying to me. "How do you know?" I asked! "What if they really are giants?"

We came to the agreement that we would make the 15-minute drive to the Boys Club and if they were in fact giants we could leave. I didn't have to play actual giants.

I agreed.

You won't believe this. They weren't actual giants.

I decided to play, scored a majority of our points again, and the team was victorious. I even got my favorite drink after the game—a Welch's Grape soda from the vending machine. It cost all of $0.25 back then, but man, did I love those things! I can still taste them now.

Less alcohol in those drinks—way more refreshing.

DAY 3

Broken Open

Lesson Learned – Distorted thinking.

I learned this term is what was taking place when I would make excuses for my drinking, like when Danielle would smoke weed early in the day, or when my heavy drinking friends would drink more than me.

It was an excuse for my behavior.

Danielle could smoke early in the morning and still be fine. Not her best version, the bright and sharp one she could have been, but still sharp enough to do what she needed to do.

I clearly can't drink and control it anymore. That's not anyone's fault but my own. I can't and shouldn't project that on anyone else.

Lowest Low – I think I've slept six hours or so in two days now. My heart races during the day, which is an experience I've never really felt before. I have a new sense of empathy for people that struggle with anxiety and stress to this degree every day. That would be unbearable.

As I mentioned, I've been living a lie for two years now. All of this is a result of me being dependent on alcohol, or more accurately, using it increasingly as a coping mechanism. That mechanism then kept me in the shitty cycle of being sad, drinking, regretting the drinking, being sad again because I drank, then drinking again because I feel sad.

Owen,

It helps me to journal my thoughts to you.

It's Day 3, and I'm already starting to learn about my failures and some of the projections I was unfairly putting on other relationships these past few months. Turns out that when I was making excuses like, "My other friends drink more than me," or when I was blaming drinking on other relationship triggers, even talking about the fact that someone like Danielle smoked weed, that's what's known as distorted thinking.

That was me trying to excuse my behaviors based on other circumstances that aren't relevant to me or the fact that I have a drinking problem. That's not fair to those other people, and more importantly, their habits have nothing to do with mine. Most of them can function with those habits and still be OK. I can't. I know that now.

On a happier note, I learned that cats lie down your stomach and purr when they feel your stress and sadness. That explains why Watson, our cat, was always so attracted to us during our difficult times. She was actually trying to heal us.

You won't remember this, but Danielle and I lost a child a few months ago. Afterward, Watson would lie on her chest all day and even at night. Watson is a healer.

My first appointment is tomorrow at noon with a therapist, and I've already filled out all my paperwork. It was really difficult to answer those questions honestly with respect to the amount of drinking I've done and how often.

The other thing that was enlightening to me was how depressed and how many negative thoughts I am having about myself and my self-worth. I think badly about myself every day now. I feel like a failure on so many fronts even though I know them not to be true. It's bizarre.

I could have been better as a father. My business is failing. I feel like I'm failing professionally.

In turn, I drank to solve what felt like depression as a coping mechanism. That was a vicious cycle. It was never going to end until I bottomed out, and that happened with Danielle leaving and bringing these things to my attention.

I've never been this low before.

The last six or seven months have been one thing after another. It's been snowballing. Unfortunately, Danielle was the recipient of a lot of those negative emotions—those negative thoughts and feelings.

The hardest part of it all is that once you get in this cycle it's extremely difficult to find your way out. I know yoga is important for me and my health. I enjoy meditating and finding that space, that peace. But when I was a drinker, especially heavier and more often toward the end, I didn't feel like doing any of those things.

That made everything worse.

It's a downward spiral. I felt bad so I should have done yoga and/or meditated, but I couldn't. I felt powerless. That's extremely difficult for someone who prides themselves on being tough, driven, intelligent, and having a really strong willpower.

Willpower, now that's a funny term in the world of sports and in life. Willpower.

What does it even mean? How do we measure it?

I apparently had amazing willpower even at a young age. I think one of my fondest and most bizarre memories of my willpower was at the age of 12. We were playing in a national basketball tournament in Salt Lake City, Utah. We were on the consolation side of the tournament.

You don't know this yet, but usually when your team is on the consolation side, the officials don't call many fouls and are focused on moving the games along quickly. Honestly, I didn't even know that until this particular game.

In basketball, you're taught not to reach for the ball to steal it from your opponent. Move your feet, stay in front of them, but don't reach. The officials will usually call a foul on you if you do.

Well, in this game, the refs weren't calling shit. So I thought why not reach? Let's see how far we can take this!

The first time my man had the ball I reached in to steal it and—wouldn't you know?—it worked. I stole the ball and went down and scored. Our coach had been trying to get us to play more aggressively, but we were slow to take him up on the encouragement. We didn't believe the referees would let us play that way.

I now believed.

A couple trips later my man was dribbling the ball up the court again. I reached and I stole the ball again. I went down and scored again.

It's really uncommon to just take the ball from your opponent like that in basketball or to steal the ball straight from them. It is rare once in a game, really rare twice, and extremely rare a third time or so I thought.

The very next trip, with our crowd cheering me on at this point for my aggressive play, my man tried to crossover dribble again. He clearly hadn't learned his lesson. I reached for the ball and knocked it away. I was going to steal the ball and score again.

My opponent thought otherwise.

With the ball knocked loose, he was going to put an end to this. He put his head down and ran straight at my face. Bam! His forehead hit my nose.

My nose was busted all to hell—broken in fact. We didn't know it at the time. Here's the willpower portion of the story.

I was the best guard on this particular team, and we were playing really well when I was in the game. With me out, it looked like we would lose.

The solution? Shove paper towels up my nose to stop the bleeding so I could return to the game and keep playing.

"Is that OK with you, son?" my dad asked from the bench.

My dad helped coach most of my athletic teams growing up. He was a great influence on my early life and athletic career and even more so later in life.

This was, ummm, not one of those moments.

"Sure, sounds fine. Let's do it." I replied.

I return to the game, and we win the game. End of story, right? Uh, no. Far from it.

A couple weeks go by, and my nose hasn't really healed yet. It's still crooked to this day. But worse than that is I kept smelling something bad. It was as though I wasn't wearing deodorant or something.

Maybe it was someone around me? The smell would come and go, but it was progressively getting worse over the days after the initial incident.

After repeatedly telling my parents of the smell and the fact that my nose is still crooked, we decide to get it checked out. The doc recommended we leave my nose as is, "Unless you're thinking about becoming a model," he said.

"But we should probably get the paper towels out of there."

That's right. I had paper towels stuck in my nose for almost two weeks. Disgusting, I know. When we were shoving them up my nose, they had torn them into tiny pieces trying to stop the bleeding. Apparently, we didn't get all the pieces out, which also explained the smell that was lingering for days, progressively getting worse.

I ended up displaying willpower during the game, in the recovery, and then in the weeks that followed in putting up with the pain and smell. That wouldn't be the last time my willpower would get me in trouble in my life.

DAY 4

Triple Playing with Pain

Lesson Learned – The book, *This Naked Mind,* talks about the physical effects of addiction. Our body blacks out as a defense mechanism because we have fucked it up so bad when we drink heavily.

Lowest Low – Owen asked where Danielle was and what was wrong with us. I told him Daddy was sick and needed help, and that Danielle won't be back around us for a while until Daddy can get better. Lots of follow-up questions ensued.

I cried in bed trying to explain what was wrong. It's hard trying to have that conversation with anyone especially your son who is not yet four.

Owen,

I've been doing a lot of research and learning more about addiction and the behaviors that exist around them. One of them being that no one can will their way through addiction. No matter how tough the mind, how strong they are mentally or physically—it's impossible. That's a really hard lesson for an accomplished athlete and coach to surrender to, to accept.

It made me realize I was trying to will others into my love too.

27

I tried to put people in a box, make them feel something I wanted instead of letting them be themselves and celebrating them. That was a pretty big awakening or mind shift for me—understanding I was trying to make my relationship with Danielle something I wanted.

I did the same thing with alcohol. That's not a healthy idea with a person, but that's a terrible idea with drugs or alcohol.

Initially, it was difficult to get over the fact that Danielle told me the unfiltered truth about my drinking and our relationship.

I felt as though someone should feel sorry for me and should be there for me. Upon further reflection, I can't imagine the strength it took for her and others to have those conversations with me.

I spoke with Lisa, a friend from my Yoga Teacher Training, for about 20 minutes today about alcohol. She recommended a book that I immediately went and picked up, *This Naked Mind*. It discusses the physical effects alcohol has on the mind and body.

The book discusses powerful facts like we black out because our body is in shock and that it does so as a defense mechanism. Damn, I've blacked out quite a few times. That's scary.

I look forward to reading and learning more. My thinking mind likes to have the science behind addiction and the negative effects it has on both the body and mind.

Earlier I was listening to a podcast about addiction, and it mentioned that great change is always preceded by chaos. That feels a bit like my life right now.

I know these next couple weeks will be incredibly challenging, but I look forward to the man I will be when I come out on the other side.

There was another great teaching point in *This Naked Mind* that says an addict's mind lives in the space between when will I get my first drink of the day and when they actually do.

I lived in that space for over two years now, almost daily. I had several long stretches of sobriety, but I found that point particularly powerful.

Oftentimes I'd wake up and wonder when I'd get my first drink. I'd think about it at work, at home, teaching yoga. When can I have my first drink today?

They say that is the worst possible place to be in life, and I must say that I agree. I lived in that space for years now; I don't ever want to be there again.

I know I will be the healthiest version of myself, mind and body, and that gives me strength.

My first appointment with my therapist is today. I was brutally honest on my intake agenda about how much I drank, how often, and how I was feeling mentally. I'm sure it will be pretty jarring to hear but it is best for me in the long run. I'm excited for that growth.

Last night you and I had a really tough conversation. This is the longest you've gone without seeing Danielle.

Lying in bed, you were sad and asked about her. I told you that Daddy is sick, and that she needs to be away from Daddy for a while. That was followed up by lots of questions on why I was sick, which was tough to explain.

I talked about the hospital again with you, my trip to the ICU, and how I needed to get help. Lots of tears in bed for me, lots of tears for the past week, and lots of emotion.

Another thing I have learned is a point Lisa made in that sometimes the most important things in our lives have to be taken away from us before we are willing to take action. That feels like what's happened to me.

I was lucky enough to not lose you; I always had that self-control. I had to lose nearly everything else to finally bottom out.

I think a lot during the day now: about my business, about teaching, and about my sobriety. I'm trying to learn and trying to grow. But you and Danielle still hold around 75 percent of my headspace right now. I think it's just the uncertainty of it all. I realize I can still have a say in what happens with the other areas of my life. That makes those things easier to process. I don't have a say in what happens with her though. That's difficult.

What brings me a smile, peace even, is I know I will be good enough for you. I also begin to see, to know that I deserve an incredible love with a partner to share this great new version of myself. That mind shift has been really powerful for the last day or so.

The empty space of no texting and talking to a partner is challenging. I've tried to fill it with meditation, yoga, and even a massage today. That seems to help even though the massage was tough as I couldn't stop my mind from racing, from thinking, from wandering about the past, the future, what has happened, and what might happen.

The opposite of a mindful mind, a meditative mind, is a monkey mind. Mind racing, heart racing, I might as well start running outside too while I'm at it and get all the pieces of my existence in some kind of heart-pounding, exhilarating, and racing type of experience.

The ironic part is we are always searching for those types of experiences as an athlete. Heart pounding, high intensity, crowd cheering type moments—like a 100-meter dash in the Olympics.

Those dreams shattered early for me. I never was much of a racer as an athlete. I always would rather have a ball or be chasing one.

It's not that running sprints mentally or physically was challenging for me. It's not that I was slow either. I was an above average runner. But I would never say I was fast.

I didn't like the suddenness of the result. Run fast for ten seconds and then win or lose. That didn't make sense to me.

However, there were those occasional moments when the stars aligned. My playing a sport where a ball was involved, and I was involved in a dead sprint, like a baseball game I was involved in around the age of 12.

I was playing on elite baseball teams now during the summer season and occasionally my friends from the Catholic school I attended would ask me to play on their team.

Their team wasn't good.

They were my friends though and that's a big deal at that age so I'd still agree to play with them from time to time. One of those days would provide a moment that put me in the local newspaper for the first time in my life.

I was playing first base, which was uncommon for the best player on a baseball team at that age.

I told you that this team wasn't very good. On this team, I was one of the only ones that would catch the ball every single time. That's how bad they were.

So instead of shortstop or centerfield, where most teams put their best and most athletic players, I was stuck at first base.

There were runners on first and second base, no outs, and I was holding the runner on first. The score is irrelevant to this story, but let's say it was 4–2, and we were winning.

Anyway, both runners attempted to steal as the pitch was made. The batter hit a line drive high over my head. I was still standing on first base holding the runner on. I jumped off of the base, high in the air, and caught the line drive. One out.

I was holding the runner on first base, but he was attempting to steal second when the pitch was made. The batter hit a line drive to me. I caught it in the air, and then landed on the base the runner on first was supposed to be on. He was now out too. Two outs.

That meant that there was only one runner left—the runner that started on second base and was stealing on the pitch trying to get to third base. I have the ball in my glove now, two outs, and a decision to make. Do I trust the guy running toward second base on my team to catch the ball as I try and throw it to him?

Remember, this team sucks.

Or do I run to second base and effectively race the guy that was trying to steal third back to second base? I chose the race.

I chose wisely.

With the ball in my glove, I started sprinting toward second base, and the runner trying to steal third didn't realize why everyone was shouting at him to go back; he was confused.

He thought he was supposed to be running toward third base; he was trying to steal! That buys me another couple seconds. I got to second base comfortably before he did to turn what is known as an unassisted triple play.

A quick Google search shows that this play is in fact more rare than a perfect game in Major League Baseball—one of the most rare plays in the game. And—wouldn't you know it?—as a result, that was the first time your dad got his name in the local newspaper.

DAY 5

Time Is Relative

Lesson Learned – There are a lot of people that do love you in your life no matter how dark or grim it may feel. You have to reach out and be open to their love. It's hard, really hard, and you have to work at relationships and love. But it's out there for you.

Lowest Low – My therapist asked me if I could start with loving myself. Could I receive self-love? I looked her straight in the eye crying and said, "No, I don't think I deserve love."

I bottomed out today and then started the climb back up.

Owen,

Yesterday was the second hardest day I've had in my recovery but also one that ended with an optimism I haven't felt in my life in some time. Today presented new opportunities and challenges, but I look forward to the experience of those challenges and beginning the real work, the real healing.

My first session yesterday with my therapist went about as expected. It was a total train wreck. I cried for over half the hour I was there—the revelatory moment 50 minutes in as she was trying to wrap up. She said the process starts with self-love and asked me if I was capable of that.

"Can you love yourself?" she asked.

I thought about it for a while and with tears in my eyes said, "No, I don't love myself. I don't think I deserve love."

She was taken aback. "What do you mean you don't deserve love?"

I said, "I'm just being honest. Look at all the things we've discussed today. My sickness, which ended my relationship with my loving partner and was directly affecting my business, sabotaging all these important pieces of my life. I don't think I deserve love from anyone including myself. That's just how I feel at the moment."

She said, "That's where the healing has to start, Ryan. You deserve love especially self-love."

Now I continue that process of healing and realizing that I am worthy of love especially from myself.

I called my mom after the session to let her know I realized now that alcohol could no longer be a part of my life. She was relieved. I think she thought I had a problem for a while and felt good that I was finally ready to admit it.

Calling my dad was emotional for different reasons. He's worked so hard on showing me healthy practices of meditation and self-love. It was hard to tell him all of that wasn't enough.

That's not true actually. Who knows where I'd be without the amount I did possess? I need to remove alcohol from the equation for it to have its desired effect. That's a better way of putting it.

Susan, the teacher that certified me to become a yoga instructor and someone that has been an incredible mentor for me this past year, has decided to help me on my sober journey as my mentor.

She's opened my eyes to some powerful things she's noticed for a while including the fact that I've been in a bad space and that I'd die if I didn't start to make some changes.

That's still hard to hear. I know it's true.

My gift to her, to Danielle, to you, and to everyone around me is the life I live every day. The real, authentic version of myself. The one that helps athletes, coaches, and people all around the world with mindfulness, meditation, yoga, and self-love.

Susan and I talked for around an hour last night. I cried a lot, again. We talked about all the healing I need to do. The reason she wants to help me is that she sees the greatness inside of me, and she knows I need to make an impact in the world.

I will impact the world. I'll create a ripple effect in the sports world.

I feel it's my life's purpose to help athletes and coaches that feel this way by helping them to stop feeling this way. I want to raise their awareness level around their mind, their emotions. How to balance them, how to accept difficult emotions, and then move on from them in a healthy, raw, and vulnerable way.

I still think of Danielle, but it's declining in intensity and frequency. I instead focus more on my healing.

I notice my mind jumping around about her, my life, and my business. From thought to thought—monkey mind as I mentioned earlier, which makes it tougher to meditate.

This process of thinking leads many to judge themselves and their practice. I instead try to think something peaceful about you or Danielle, someone that I feel love for, then I focus on returning to the breath. Returning to me.

Susan talked about that later with my journaling too.

I took Susan's class this morning and cried during the ending, what's known as savasana, for ten or so straight minutes. She kneeled next to me with her hand on my chest telling me to breathe.

It can be so overwhelming thinking of the pain I've caused Danielle and others. How can I focus on myself when I know I'd be spiraling toward an impending death without others pushing me to this point? How can I focus on myself knowing how much I hurt people along the way? I did some dark things as I was feeding my ego, my bad wolf as I call it.

I know the answer. I need to start with myself, build day by day, love myself, and then start to address the other areas down the road. Susan suggested some mantras to stay present, then writing your name down, or Danielle's, and what I'm feeling at that moment—just one or two words like Danielle – Forgiveness or Owen – Love.

I went to an AA meeting tonight to explore that process and line of thinking. The session went well. It was all older guys with some pretty rough lives. Cheating on their wives, wives kicking them out, bad relationships with their children, alcohol and drugs taking over their lives—the stories were rough to hear. That would have happened to me too. I'm glad I had the strength, support, self-love, self-confidence, and the help of others to act when I did.

As I head to the city I grew up in later in the evening I realize how great it will be to be back—back to where it all began for me in life and as an athlete. I will admit the last 72 hours or so have moved so slowly that it's a needed relief.

Time feels like it's crawling along. Minutes feel like hours. I've noticed that happens in life, both ways, speeding up and slowing down.

What is it that Einstein says about time and its relativity? "Put your hand on a hot stove for a minute, and it seems like an hour. Sit with a pretty girl for an hour, and it seems like a minute. That's relativity."

That's so true. These past few days have felt like weeks.

It's true in athletics too. It can take years for you to break through, or you can go from nothing to something in the blink of an eye. Usually, it's a combination of the two.

Lionel Messi has a great quote on this. He said, "It took me 17 years and 114 days to become an overnight success." I understand what he means.

Years and years of work then pay off in a moment, a game. That's how my basketball career took off. I remember it well.

I played on a highly competitive traveling team from when I was 10 years old through high school. I always started on those teams and was always one of our best players. Most of those traveling team teammates started or played on varsity at their respective high schools as freshmen. I was stuck on the freshmen team.

As a sophomore, I started on JV but still couldn't break through. We played our games right before the varsity on most nights. I remember thinking, knowing, I was better than the guards in front of me. I just needed a chance.

Before a home game one night, the senior homecoming queen, Jarron, was standing by me for the national anthem. I was having another one of these frustrated moments thinking to myself how it was bullshit I was stuck on JV. I glanced at Jarron admiring her and her beauty.

In the moment between my thinking about how I should be playing and admiring her beauty, she caught me looking at her and stared back into my eyes. She smiled.

I was holding a fountain drink, a small 12 ounce cup. Once she smiled at me, my hand went numb, and I dropped the cup. My drink spilled everywhere. Again, this was during the national anthem so it was totally quiet. It was like a scene from a movie, a bad high school romcom or something.

Jarron apologized saying, "Sorry if I made you drop your drink."

How embarrassing!

Two weeks later, still stuck on JV, we were playing a team our varsity usually beat every season. I scored 16 points in the JV game and played well. I was clearly the best player in the city at the JV level, and it wasn't particularly close. Our varsity would go on to lose to that bad opponent after our JV game.

And just like that, when I went to practice the next day, my JV head coach told me I'd be starting varsity at point guard for the rest of the season effective immediately.

I went from JV to starting varsity overnight, literally. I fucking killed it too.

In my first start I went 0–4 from the free throw line and scored 0 points. We lost to a team that our high school hadn't lost to in 25 years. (Can you pick up sarcasm in the writing?)

Anyway, to our coach's credit, he stuck with me. I started every game for the rest of the season, and we upset one of the best teams in city's history in the postseason that year to win the district championship. The defense I played on their best scorer was a big reason for our win.

Remember Jarron? The girl who caused me to drop my drink with just a smile? We started dating about halfway through that season. A beautiful girl, a senior, a cheerleader, and the literal homecoming queen started dating me as a sophomore in high school once I got called up to varsity.

That was my first taste of celebrity life and the benefits of what my athletic career would provide me. Would Jarron have dated me if I didn't play sports and if I didn't have that incredible ascent all of a sudden? Maybe but I doubt it.

It's not that she was shallow. She was a great and kind person actually. But you just get a spotlight shined on you as you start to succeed on the court or field depending on your sport. For me that was always basketball.

It opened doors that normally wouldn't be opened and started conversations I wouldn't normally get to have with people that normally wouldn't talk to me.

Sports can do that for you too, someday, if that's what you would like. You just have to be careful with that side of athletics just like you have to do with alcohol.

They are similar in that way, both providing extreme highs and lows. The only difference is the highs in sports are real, raw, and genuine. Alcohol feels real at the time, but it fades, doesn't last, and is fake.

You'll see how as we go.

DAY 6

A Moment

Lesson Learned – I always looked at relationships to make me feel fulfilled. When they no longer serve that purpose, I sabotage them. Relationships won't make me happy; I have to make myself happy.

Lowest Low – As stated in *This Naked Mind*, alcohol has the worst rating by far of all drugs—with a harm rating of 72. Heroin is next with 55, and crack follows with a 54. Why the fuck was I drinking so hard for so long again?

Owen,

Today is Friday, and it finally feels like I am done with the bottoming out part of this thing. I know it will come in waves, highs and lows, but it feels like I am starting to see a light inside of me again that I haven't felt in a while.

I taught two yoga classes this morning, and it feels so much better to not be bullshitting my way through classes, surviving off of talent, like

39

I did for the past six months. I've been putting thought into my flows and themes, taking time to create the playlists. I can tell my students are enjoying the renewed energy and love what I am passing on to them. It feels nice to be back.

After class, I lifted weights for the first time in months. My body didn't hurt. I know this is due to the emotional weight being lifted more than the physical pain I experienced. Even my shoulder felt better. Earlier, it would always hurt when I would try to bench-press, but today I got through it just fine. That relationship we have between mind and body is truly amazing.

I've been eating mostly fruit, and that's really leaned me up. It's shocking what happens to the body when you don't drink every day. My only abstinences from alcohol were when I was around you. You were always more important than alcohol. I could toe that line and stop around you. I feel joy, I feel pride, and I find peace in that.

A friend brought up a good point about this to me when I told him that I was sober now, and that I didn't drink around you. He said, "That probably should have been a sign to you. The disconnect of who you knew you should be around your son, and who you were for yourself." I had never thought of it like that.

Danielle and I spoke for the first time through email. I felt a sense of relief to write and tell her, even briefly, that I know and see what I have done. There will be a time for me to apologize for everything and then see what's next for us both right away and then in the future. Now is not that time.

The guys from that AA meeting yesterday all reached out at different points today. It's been nice to have a support system in place. I see the benefits of AA for others even though I don't agree with most things philosophically.

I still choose to not list myself as an alcoholic and hammer all the negatives like *I'm powerless over alcohol*. It seems like a dark way to look at the situation. I disagree with that statement. My power is in the ability to stop with the help of others—to know that it's not beneficial to drink anymore and that something has to change in my lifestyle.

My mentor suggested an alternative, *"I'm sick, and I need help, mentally and emotionally."* I can't drink anymore, and honestly, I don't want to. Alcohol feels like it's sucking the soul and the spirit out of me. That's why it got the name "spirits" originally. I like my spirit. I'd prefer to hold on to it while I'm still here.

On my drive to Springfield to spend time with your grandpa, I started listening to a podcast on addiction. Your grandpa's house has always been so grounding for me. His energy and all the plants he has—there's good vibes there. While he's not the most emotional guy. He's very balanced, listens really well, and always offers incredible perspective to me and my situation.

The biggest moment of the day for me was on the drive down, however. I was listening to that podcast on addiction, and at the very end a female on the podcast began speaking into her past relationships while she was still drinking.

She mentioned that she always looked for her partner to make her happy, to provide her with the love in their relationship. And when the partner could no longer do that, she would sabotage the relationship or just move on. The problem was no relationship could provide that to her because she didn't love herself because of her drinking. It was a vicious cycle for her because of her lack of self-love and her lack of acceptance.

That's what I did to Danielle in our relationship for the past few months. Hearing that, I was thinking, "Oh shit, that was me this whole time!"

I plan on reading some more from my books today and tonight while I am at your Papa's house. That's all I plan on doing really. Journaling, writing, reading, yoga, meditating, swimming, and eating some fire food from back in Springfield.

I ate at Pizza House tonight with my dad. You love their pizza because the pieces are really small, about one inch by one inch. I think we had it last time we were down here. I also went and saw all of Papa's flowers, meditated by his fountains, and watched kids play on the swing next door. It's beautiful.

I did some writing and reading tonight but just a little. Dad and I mostly sat on the porch and talked, catching up on what all was going on with me the past week or so. It's been a long week and a half as you know.

My dad has become such a good listener that it's nice to be able to sit there and talk with him and sometimes just sit there in silence. Neither of us spoke, comfortable in silence.

The one chapter I did get to today from *The Naked Mind* was pretty frustrating but good to understand now why I was thinking and acting the way I was the past few months with Danielle.

It is called "You Polluted," and it talks directly about the negative effects of the drug alcohol. First of all, it has the worst rating of all drugs, with a harm rating of 72. Then, next is heroin with a harm score of 55, and crack cocaine was third with a harm score of 54. That's pretty unbelievable, but that's not what jumped out to me personally about my behaviors.

"You Polluted" also talked about how it slows down your neural highways including the cerebellum, which is responsible for coordination, memory (mine was starting to fade), and, most importantly, my emotional responses.

I think of some of the fights I had with my former partners, and I just shake my head now. If I had been more present, more empathic, and, most importantly, sober I just can't imagine how those most likely float away and don't even become an issue.

How I could and should have told former partners like Danielle, "Don't worry about it," or "How can I help?" which I see now but couldn't in the moment. It's not that I didn't want to make it work. I was trying, but I just finally see now that I couldn't because my brain and emotions were shot.

That's saddening and frustrating, but all I can do now is apologize when the time is right from the bottom of my heart. I hope I have the chance to show Danielle and whoever else what a sober version of me will look like when that time comes and then move forward.

Being cloudy, foggy, and living in that haze is no fun in life; it's even less so in sports. There are a couple times in particular I remember feeling cloudy or foggy as an athlete—none really from alcohol. Well, maybe once in college actually. We'll save that story for later. It's a good one.

I do remember being in a fog in a huge game in high school.

Believe it or not, I played on one of the best high school basketball teams in Missouri state history. My Kickapoo Chiefs were 28–1 heading into the Elite 8 game of my junior year in high school. I was the starting point guard on this team. Although I wasn't the leading scorer on the team, I was the most important piece of the puzzle to our team as I made the team go.

I'd later be recognized as such by being named first-team all-state as a junior in Missouri in the biggest class in the state at the time, 4A. It was extremely rare to make first-team all-state as a junior. It had only happened once in school history up to that point. I was the second in our school's 25-year history.

But back to the fog.

We were playing Jefferson City, and our scouts had labeled them as a football school that had a couple good basketball players on the roster too. That was, ummm, a bit of an understatement in hindsight. Who were those football players that happened to be playing basketball that our scouts were referencing?

One was Justin Gage who was a 6'6 point guard and went on to play both basketball and football at Missouri. He played wide receiver in the NFL for a number of years mostly with the Tennessee Titans and Chicago Bears.

Another one of those football players was Justin Smith. He was a five-time NFL Pro-Bowler, five-time All Pro defensive end, and two-time first-team All Pro.

The point being, these dudes were a little more talented than "football guys," playing basketball. They were world-class athletes. Luckily, we didn't know that at the time.

Jefferson City also had another player who would go on to play high-level Division I football at Missouri and a couple more who would go on to play Division II basketball and have good careers. They were a really talented team.

I was our best player and I would go on to be a good Division II basketball player. Athletically, it was a bit of a mismatch looking back, but at the time, we were actually ranked #2 in the state of Missouri, well ahead of Jefferson City.

Now to the game. Not surprisingly, it was back and forth, tight all the way. I was playing well. Then at one point late in the game there was a loose ball on the ground. I was always a claw and scratch for every inch toughness-type of player so I dove into the pile and tried to get the ball. One of the other gigantic football players got it instead.

As the bodies cleared and well after the whistle, I felt something catch the top left side of my eye. Someone had caught me with a late elbow. It was to the left of my eye, close to my temple. Things became foggy.

I stumbled around for a bit and went and sat on the wrong bench trying to get my bearings. Imagine that happening today, a basketball player going and sitting on the wrong bench because they were so disoriented. They would definitely not be allowed back in the game.

The head coach of our team thought the same thing. He assumed I was done. Jefferson City smelled blood with me—our team's point guard out of the game. They threw on a full court press and got two quick turnovers that resulted in easy scores for them. What had been a two-point lead for us turned into a four-point deficit within two minutes. Coach called a time-out.

Meanwhile, I am on the correct bench now (baby steps!) and our trainer asks me if I know where I'm at. You may laugh, but that's actually how they determined if you could reenter the game back then. They'd ask you a couple questions like what's two plus two or if you know your name. If you got the answer right, you got to go back in the game. It's hilarious to think that's how we operated only 20 years ago, but it's true.

The trainer asks me if I know where I am at now that I'm on the correct bench and I say, "Yeah, we're getting our ass kicked in the biggest game of my life."

The trainer says, "Yep! He's good to go!"

I didn't even ask my head coach if I could go back in. I just checked in. You didn't do that back then, but the press was killing our team. So I didn't ask. I just checked back in for our backup point guard.

I'd learn later that the head coach was shocked I went back in and that he hadn't used a time-out sooner because he assumed I was done for the game.

We'd claw our way back into the game and with us down one now late in the fourth quarter, we chose to foul their point guard, Justin Gage. We were hoping that he'd miss a free throw, and we'd have a chance to tie the game. He did.

In the process of him missing his free throw attempt I was blocking him out, and he came over my back committing a pushing foul. That was also his fifth foul. He has just fouled out.

We were now down two points, and I had a one and one free throw attempt meaning if I made the first, I got to shoot a second free throw potentially tying the game.

I was a decent free throw shooter but not great. But I usually made them when they counted. As I mentioned, I was the best player on our team, and I was confident stepping to the line even though I had most likely been concussed about 20 minutes before that.

I step to the line, and the first attempt is up. It glances the rim and goes in. We're down one. I make the next one, and the game is now tied. We have the advantage as Gage has just fouled out. Things look good for us.

I we miss, we have to continue fouling hoping they miss a free throw again so we can score to tie or take the lead.

The second attempt is up. It hits the front of the rim again, but this time it kicks a little harder to the back of the rim. It bounces once more, twice more, and lips off the side of the rim. I missed.

In my attempt, the ball had hit the rim four times on a single shot and then eventually rolled off and out. We had to start fouling again. To their credit, they would go six for six from the free throw line down the stretch, and that would be as close as we'd get the rest of the game.

We lost by two.

ason ended as still one of the best in Kickapoo history at 28–2.
d up first-team all-Ozarks and first-team all-state, more of a
how I played in big moments as opposed to my statistics that
season. But it wouldn't be enough to get us a state title. The temporary
fog proved to be too much to overcome.

The more I reflect on that moment, even on that last sentence, the
more I realize that's not true. It's not one moment in life, one play, one
fight, or one action we take that defines us. It's a series of moments really.
In sports, in relationships, and in our lives everything is tied together.

The power is in our ability to learn from these things that happen in
our past and to stay present in those moments that challenge us—those
foggy moments. If we learn from our mistakes and surround ourselves
with good people who care about us then those foggy moments aren't so
bad. Those foggy moments don't last as long.

But if we live in the past, dwell on our mistakes, and surround
ourselves with shitty people then the fog can last a lot longer. That's
where mindfulness, self-awareness, and self-love become so important.
If we're not careful, that cloud, that fog can follow us for longer stretches
of a basketball game and a 6–0 run becomes a 20–4 run.

That fog, that darkness can and will follow you in life too. What should
be a bad few weeks or a bad few months can turn into a bad few years.
Practice those good habits and always strive to find that self-love and
self-awareness. Surround yourself with good teammates. And by doing
so, you'll avoid the fog.

DAY 7

Liquid Discourage

"IF YOU'RE JUST SAFE ABOUT THE CHOICES YOU MAKE, YOU DON'T GROW."
—HEATH LEDGER, ACTOR

Lesson Learned – Alcohol doesn't give you liquid courage or improve your sexual performance. It makes you dumber and less courageous. It makes the sex less enjoyable and less sensual especially for girls. Alcohol is fun, and that's why people use it. But it's also wildy romanticized with movies, music, and other platforms. Most of our experiences aren't heightened instead they are deadened with the use of alcohol.

Positive Moment – Reflecting back on a pendant I rediscoverd in my bathroom drawer, what it meant for me now, and what it means moving forward. Ganesha, the remover of obstacles, the sign of a new beginning had been hiding in plain sight. Putting a necklace around her, the pendant, and putting it on my neck made me feel good, feel calm.

Owen,

The morning started around 9 a.m., and Dad and I sat outside for around an hour. I read a couple of the chapters from the AA's book—the Big Book they call it. That continues to be tough to swallow not because I don't think I have a problem; I know I do. Even though it's not at the level of the examples they use in the book.

47

The problem I have is just with the negativity and the lack of control they keep labeling us all with. It goes against everything that I have learned with my past training about being kind, forgiving, and staying positive with ourselves and with our thinking.

You essentially admit you are powerless against alcohol and that you give in to a higher power to solve your problem with alcohol. I believe in God, and I know I have a problem. I just need to work around the phrasing so that I can figure out how to be comfortable with the process. The dichotomy of it all is that your current line of thinking, your current awareness has gotten you exactly where you are in life—dependent on something you shouldn't be dependent on. So you need to shift your thinking and behaviors to change that. I am aware of that.

But there is also a balance there in that not everything I have done is bad, not all of my habits and lines of thinking are bad. In fact, I'd take that a step further and say most of them are good, are healthy. It's just my mind or learning disability around my learned behaviors having to do with alcohol that needs to change. That makes it really hard for me to blindly accept or listen to any person or program. In AA they ask you to do that. At least, it feels that way right now.

As I want to be all in with this and getting better, I know I need to figure all this out as we go so that I can be sure I am better on the other side in the next few weeks into the next few years and eventually the rest of my life. This recovery process will be more like a great jazz song I assume. It ebbs and flows, some parts rehearsed and some parts improvised.

I went shopping for a necklace for a pendant I've had for a while. I posted this on social media, but I wanted to share it with you. Below is the story of where my mind went throughout the day and reflecting back on the experience.

(There's an interesting story about this pendant. It's a symbol of eastern religion that's known as Ganesha, or the remover of obstacles and the symbol of new beginnings.

I bought this on a retreat in Hungary and didn't really know why. Our entire group was practicing yoga and they had this charm on the end of a set of mala beads. The studio had all kinds of items for sale in their store including these beads. Those that know me know that I have a ton of mala beads and don't need more, but I couldn't walk away. I felt an energy about it, an attraction.

I bought the beads and pendant, but the weight of it made the beads too heavy to wear on my wrist. So I took only the charm off at the time thinking I'd buy a necklace soon and start wearing it again.

Fast forward a year and my life was starting to get really challenging mostly due to my decisions. I'm starting to pack up for the weekend and when I look at the bottom of a basket in my bathroom, it sat there. It was in great condition—a little flawed but ready. Just sitting there by itself. It feels like that has been my potential this past year too.

Sitting there, untapped, and waiting to be discovered again—waiting to be used in a way that takes advantage of my strengths. So I picked it up on Friday back in Overland Park, and today I bought a necklace for it and will wear it every day to help me remove the obstacles in my life. The necklace now representing a new beginning, a time to start realizing my potential, and to do what I was made to do. I will help train and heal athletes, mentally and physically, who have been through some of the struggles that I have already faced. And to help them face the ones I've never seen before.

Taking accountability on my side is where that journey starts, and I'm starting to do that in a number of areas of my life. It feels great. Self-love is the hardest for me. I'm so demanding and critical of myself and others that I can be tough to love. It's tough for me to love myself let alone other people. But I'm committed to change that. And now, I also have people holding me accountable to that. I'm thankful for that.

Here's to removing obstacles and to new beginnings :)

The few chapters I read today from *This Naked Mind* really hit home again. I am thoroughly enjoying this book. Today's chapters were on the common misconceptions of how alcohol gives us courage, makes us better in bed, and then a chapter called "Oh Shit, We're Stuck."

The first two chapters are pretty self-explanatory, but the interesting part of those chapters is that it actually does the opposite. It makes you less courageous and dumber when you need courage. It makes the sexual experience worse for both partners but especially for females when they drink. (Remember this as you get older!) The ironic part of the sex chapter is, as I reflect back on my sexual experiences, that the best sex I usually had with a partner was totally sober or else in the morning when we both first woke up and were sober.

This clarity allows me to promise myself to be better now, not drink, and learn from these mistakes. I promise to continue to practice self-love, self-discipline, empathy, and love toward you; moving forward for you in whatever way I can.

I want to be here now to support you and help you out however I can as an incredible father. Please know that I'm incredibly proud of you right now and will be proud of you moving forward too. You're beautiful, you're amazing, and you're going to be incredibly successful in life. Not just as a son or as a partner for someone eventually but at whatever else you decide to take on in life. I can't wait to see what that looks like for you.

Success will come for you just like it did for me. Oftentimes, through adversity in your life. In your athletic career and in your life there will be times that don't seem to make sense, that will leave you asking why things happen to you. These periods can last days; they can last weeks; they can last months. They always pass.

Our first basketball game during my senior season of high school was supposed to be a break out party for me. No more sharing the limelight this year as I would be under the intense spotlight. The team was now mine, and I was going to relish in that role. Coming off of that 28–2 season and returning only one other part-time starter from last year's team it was going to be challenging, but I was up for it.

I was never a cocky player. I didn't think I was the man and didn't beat my chest when I played. I was quiet, played hard, and was physical. I led by example. But this year was going to be the first time in my career that I clearly needed to be the leading scorer of my team. I needed to take the most shots on the team. That would be new to me and would prove to be difficult. I didn't enjoy that mentality.

The first game was against a really good opponent. One of the best teams in the state of Arkansas, Springdale High School. They had a good 6'6 guard. I had battled him for years on the AAU circuit. They also possessed a mammoth of a man who was 6'10 and would go on to play football, offensive line, at the University of Arkansas. What is it with me and playing against giant football players? I just realized that.

It was a back and forth most game, neither of us really separated much, but the biggest play of the game was when I fell and landed on my left hand. It would end up being a hairline fracture. We lost the game that night too. A great start to my senior year.

That could have been deflating for me, ruining my senior season. Instead, I didn't miss a game. They put a soft cast on there, and I could play comfortably with it using my nonshooting hand. We won our next 11 games.

The highlight was a Christmas tournament in Kansas City, Missouri at a school named William Jewell. They have a prestigious holiday tournament there—three divisions with one winner in each division.

On three consecutive nights, I'd score 17, 26, and 31 points. The last game I'd ended up with 10 assists too. I was the tournament MVP. Things were looking up for me, and I was putting my name on the map as we were knocking off high level opponents along the way.

The pendulum swung back the other way after the midpoint. We added a player at semester that disoriented our team chemistry. This circles back to my fragile mindset. This new player, Tyrone, was really good, but he needed a lot of shots. That meant other players now took less shots and scored less points.

I didn't like the fact that my teammates were frustrated with their point totals, and their shot attempts. I became hesitant on the court too. After an 11–1 start, we'd limped to a 7–10 finish.

We ended the season 18–11 and in disappointing fashion—a buzzer beater on a fluke play where an opposing player who was 0-8 shooting on the night ended up with the ball in his hands on the last play of the game. He shot it, and it swished through as the buzzer sounded. I collapsed instantly on the court that last game, and I lay there for what felt like 20 minutes. It was probably closer to two. One of my AAU coaches came and picked me up.

But that's sports. And the truth of it all is that that's life too, son. With a broken hand, thinking my season is over; an 11-1 start thinking I was one of the best players in the country; then settling in the middle of all that with a decent record but without any Division I offers to show for it like I had hoped. All of those experiences led me right where I needed to be at that time, which would then lead me right to where I am today.

That's mindfulness, and that's staying present. Success? That's all in the eye of the beholder. I see that now. Who defines your success, or what that even means is up to you. Similar to trying to define what's right and what's wrong so much of that has to do with perspective. It's just like how we started this book. That's why you hear the eastern culture talk about the right path vs. success or failure.

Are you trying to do the right thing? Was your decision-making based on pure intentions, sound mind, and sound thinking? This is true again in sports and in life. The right path will lead to happiness and inner peace for you (the athlete) and in life.

I know this too in just one week of being sober. I feel so much better. I feel cleaner and smarter quite possibly for the first time since right around the time I am referencing here. I know this is the path I need to be on. A path that will lead to success for me again in life—the right path and inner peace.

Week 2

Escape

DAY 8

A Glimpse of the End

"FOR PEOPLE WHO DRINK TOO MUCH, THE PROBLEM ISN'T REALLY
ABOUT BOOZE. IT'S ABOUT AN INABILITY TO DEAL WITH LIFE... WHAT
GIVING UP BOOZE DOES IS ALLOW YOU TO LOOK AT YOURSELF THROUGH
AN UNTAINTED MIRROR FOR THE FIRST TIME."
—COLIN FARRELL, ACTOR

Lesson Learned – Alcohol controls your emotions, causes irritability and unhappiness, attacks the memory, and your ability to process emotions. It explains the ups and downs I experienced the past few years.

Lowest Low – Driving past the place I fought with Danielle over the Fourth of July. She sat and cried in the car while Owen and I walked around looking for fireworks. The Fourth would signify the beginning of the end of our relationship.

Owen,

Today started off rocky. I've been working out two or three times a day now to quiet the mind. That has helped.

But *This Naked Mind* has been both great and really hard to read. What alcohol does to the brain, robbing it of the ability to control emotions, explains a lot as to why I'd see waves in my emotional control. Not only does it change the way your motor system works but it also attacks the area that monitors your memories and emotions. This is why alcohol causes unhappiness and irritability that only those that were intensely close to me would see, more often toward the end.

I was always coming up or coming down from these bouts with alcohol, high or low. Or my body was trying to process these emotions sober and was struggling with that irritability once I was clean. It was a vicious cycle.

It also explains why I was having so many problems with simple things recently like remembering names and conversations. It can take weeks or months for the damage of alcohol to wear off the mind.

I've felt so cloudy and foggy for months now—even years. I used to be so smart and funny, charming and witty. I've felt like Frodo with the ring around his neck for the past year as I've been unable to get rid of my precious alcohol. I finally threw that bitch into the volcano last week.

The light can and will come back to me, for me. I can feel that, and I am so excited for it—to be healthy and happy again.

It has been one week from my last drink. Although I ended up drinking on this night last week after I didn't get to see Danielle like I had anticipated. That was the final straw of my drinking, and I haven't drank since.

I've seen some pretty terrible shit over my life, things that have had a lasting effect on me. I say all of that because I think this was the toughest week of my life from start to finish. I was a 10 out of 10 on the freaking the fuck out scale on Monday. I was anxious. I couldn't sleep or eat wanting to fix everything even though I could not fix anything. I bottomed out as they say.

Then today, a week later, that tension and that stress is back down to a 5 or so. It comes in waves.

Take this morning for example. Peacefully, I got up and read some more of *The Naked Mind*, swam, and watched baseball. I had a great morning and afternoon. But then the drive back was tough as I was alone with my thoughts.

I listened to the audio book of AA, the Big Book, and it's still a tough read/listen not because I'm fighting it or I won't drink today but because it's just tough to hear some of the phrasing and teachings—all the negativity.

The most triggering part was driving by the place where I argued with Danielle on the Fourth of July when you were with us. It wasn't anything wild or loud or anything like that. I don't argue like that; I'm quite the opposite. I don't like to raise my voice or yell. I wouldn't do that with your mom either. I just make it obvious I'm done talking about something and disagree. I can be cutting and incisive in that way when I talk to someone.

I did that with Danielle on this night. It hurt her.

Driving back made me sad and angry at myself as it was all over nothing. Well, not nothing. No fight is over nothing. You'll learn that even silly fights are triggered by something in one person or the other's conscious or unconscious mind. Maybe I was unconsciously arguing with her because I wanted the relationship to fail or end—maybe both?

Most of Danielle and my fights were over inconsequential things in the grand scheme of our relationship, of life even. I don't even know what started it or how it got to that point on this particular day.

Well, it was largely because of my drinking. I was agitated that we had miscommunicated and that was coupled with the fact that I wasn't drinking, and it all made me irritable. I remember Danielle sitting in the car crying while you and I went inside. You then asked me what's wrong with Danielle, and I had to say she was just sad. That breaks my heart now.

In hindsight, it was because I was on this mission to try and find cool fireworks for you since that's our special holiday together. I get you every Fourth of July according to our parenting plan. But little did I know that Danielle had already bought some, and I was just being a dick.

I know I have to forgive myself and let it go eventually. It's these little things that pop up like that from over the course of the failed relationship that make me sad. They make my days wave up and down. That's the part where I have to heal, forgive myself, and, when the time is right, apologize.

One of the nicest parts of being back with my dad was it allowed me to heal some of the athletic trauma that I've been blocking for years now, some for decades. I also reflect on the waves of my career—waves like I've been feeling lately, emotionally.

Trauma in my sports life over dumb shit, like the fight I had with Danielle, start to rise emotionally to the surface. I reflect on the waves in my performance much like my emotions.

Trauma and waves would sum up my college career. Take my sophomore season at Southwest Baptist University as exhibit A. I'd mostly float around thinking I was better than everyone at that level when I wasn't even starting full time yet.

Waves include the time when we played Oral Roberts University early on that season. I had 0 points in the first half and 16 points in the second half. That was all mental. Why the waves? I didn't start the first half and was pissed. I was pouting. In the second half, the coach started me, and so I played like it. That has nothing to do with the coach; that's on me.

Trauma includes instances like a couple months later when the other point guard on the team, my best friend on the team, Greg Germany, died in a car crash on the way back from my hometown of Springfield, Missouri. We had been at the club on a Saturday night but since I was from Springfield and dating a cheerleader at the time I stayed in town. I was lucky; Greg wasn't. He ended up dead that night at the age of 21.

The rest of the season would be a cycle of waves and trauma. I think we lost 6 straight after Greg died. I was probably drunk for most of that time not knowing how to handle the loss of a good friend and the fact that I was better than most of the guys on my team without trying. I got benched one more time not starting again a couple more games.

I'd alternate between being pissed off at my teammates when I wasn't doing shit myself and then playing well to show them how good I could be when I was right in mind and body.

But that peace has to come from within, and I was a long way away from that. I'm still trying to find that now.

That peace can't come from others telling you how great you are; it can't come from starting or not starting; and it can't come from the results of one game or one half. And it damn sure can't come from alcohol.

You want to find peace in times of trauma? You want to help calm the waves of the mind and of life? That sanctuary, that peace is within you. Learn to harness it.

I love you.

One week down—one day at a time.

DAY 9

Open Palm

Lesson Learned – Hold anything worth having in life, anything that's genuinely good and healthy for us with an open palm. We must hold all our relationships, emotions, and athletic careers lightly and be open to the fact that things we love will come and go. What's meant to be will remain in a loving way, and what no longer serves us will leave.

Lowest Low – When discussing past relationships, I said to Susan, "None of our fights were big ones."

Susan responded, "How do you know how you made her feel or what was big to her? Lots of these little fights may have been big deals to her."

Owen,

Exactly one week sober today. I feel strong in body and mind, taught a great class today, and then took a yoga class from Susan at noon at a local studio.

Afterward, she and I met for around two hours, and I cried some pretty powerful tears and had some emotional breakthroughs. One of the most staggering was that I'm 39 years old and haven't experienced a healthy relationship in my entire life. I've seen some in passing from time to time. My dad has a lovely partner who complements him nicely. They do well together. That's one, for example.

But my parents' relationship while I was growing up and then all of my relationships to this point have all been unhealthy and filled with either deceit, alcohol, cheating, or all of the above. That was staggering to realize.

I realize too how powerful my parents' divorce has been on me both emotionally and relationship-wise. Two specific incidents, one with both my mom and dad, jumped out to me as Susan asked me to reflect on my past, and what I was really burying and couldn't let go.

The first incident? My mom slapped me during a family conversation when I brought up her cheating. I was being a smart-ass to her. She was tired of it, we all were tired of it, and I got slapped as a result.

The second? My dad challenged me to a fight in our front yard over some grass clippings. He was mad and had no one to take it out on. I was the helpless puppy in the front yard he tried to take it out on. I wouldn't have it.

The details of both of these stories aren't as important as the overarching theme. Both my parents were in pain and didn't know how to handle themselves. Their relationship was now toxic.

Worst of all was that this type of relationship now appeared normal to me. Cheating, fighting, and drinking—all these were not encouraged, but those behaviors existed. I carried those behaviors into my relationships.

The best example I have of this as a college athlete, and please don't consider this bragging, was when I was dating a beautiful girl, Cassie, during my junior year in college. Cassie and I had been on and off for over a year. She played basketball at SBU as well, and she was actually better than I was comparatively.

As I usually did when she and I were in our off periods, I started to talk to another girl. This girl, Robyn, was beautiful physically but not as good a fit for me as Cassie.

Robyn and I were on and off opposite Cassie and I. I thought I could keep their paths from crossing long enough that neither would know better until I had made my decision of who I wanted to date long term.

Eventually, their paths crossed. They figured it out and wanted to talk unbeknownst to me.

I came home from practice one day, and they were both sitting there on my couch at my apartment.

Fuck.

I walked right past them and into my bedroom. I didn't talk to either of them. I locked my door until they both left. Eventually, I lied about what was going on with the other one to both of them and somehow it was convincing enough that Cassie and I would end up dating again for another year after that. Unsuccessfully, as you might have guessed.

The point of the story with my parents and with my dating escapades over the years is that those behaviors in life, on the court and in your relationships, will always catch up with you. You'll usually get what you deserve. That's commonly known as The Law of Attraction.

It takes work in a smart, healthy, and intentional way.

You also have to be very aware of who you are surrounding yourself with and what type of behaviors you are observing and then mirroring as you go. That's eventually who, or what, you and your relationships will become.

Growing up and until this day, at the age of 39, I didn't know, see, or experience a healthy relationship. I mirrored those unhealthy behaviors my entire life. Those behaviors stop today.

I know I won't be perfect. I'll still make mistakes in love and in life. But I will be intentional about who I surround myself with, the types of behaviors and relationships I observe and interact with, and who I let into my life.

As a result, I know I'll find the kind of love and happiness I long for as a partner. I'll be the same loving and supportive person for them in return.

I can't wait to figure out what that looks like. Whether that ends up being Danielle or if it's too late for that is still to be determined. For the first time in my life, however, I have no doubt it will happen for me, for us.

DAY 10

The Calm

Lesson Learned – I reached out to Danielle on social media today, and I don't know if that was smart or not. It's so hard balancing between wanting to stay in contact with her, being in her life, and healing in my own space right now.

Lowest Low – This was a combination of a high and low today, perhaps a shift in mindset which is good. Danielle mentions that I could always let things go quicker with Owen because I love him unconditionally. I know how to move on and fix the situation without dwelling on it.

Imagine if we treated all of our relationships with loved ones with unconditional love. That's powerful.

Owen,

I went to a new meeting today. The man that runs it has a military background and a history with drugs and alcohol. I'd imagine that to be pretty common within the military. I base that off of nothing but being so isolated from friends and family. Seeing such dark shit I can only imagine the types of behaviors it pushes people toward.

I've always seen the military as the life and death version of sports in terms of the intensity, camaraderie, being ultra-competitive. The difference, obviously, is they actually have to deal with life and death. Our life and death was only wins and losses.

He runs the meeting smoothly, a topic meeting, which means someone from the group picks a topic, and we start to discuss how that's become relevant in our life. We offer advice to them or simply just speak out on it to heal. Today's topic is taking the loving-kindness and empathy we feel for others in recovery home with us to our personal lives.

The lady that brings up the topic has a lot going on at home. She's in recovery, has two adult kids in recovery, and it sounds like she also has a husband who needs to be in recovery when he's ready for it. That's a lot to digest on a daily basis especially in a healthy way.

She brings up a good point though. It's amazing how we differ in the way we treat people who we don't really know versus the ones we care the most about. Taken a step further, it would mean the ones we care about versus the ones we love unconditionally—like I do with you.

Danielle mentioned that once in passing, but she didn't mean it to be anything offensive or negative. I asked why we were going back and forth one day, and why I'm able to move on from those emotions quicker with you as compared to her.

"You love him unconditionally," she said without even skipping a beat. It took my breath away.

That was one of those moments that makes so much sense to someone who's not in the picture. It should have been apparent to me as to why I love and move on from emotions so much quicker with you, my son, and then why I didn't do so more quickly with a partner or, hell, even myself.

That's a big learning point for me today—to love myself unconditionally just like I do with you. How many of us love ourselves unconditionally like we do with those we love the most in our lives?

You've been a really calming presence this past week. You're loving and full of energy and happiness. Yes, you can be emotional or moody at times like all toddlers can be, but it would be nice if we all could be a little more childlike in most of our behaviors.

Imagine if we moved on from our emotions as quickly as toddlers do. Imagine if we were naturally curious like a toddler, exploring things and asking questions. The knowledge and potential that children your age possess, especially you, is amazing. I'm happy to be able to flame those curious and learning types of behaviors for you.

Now begins the healing for me or rather continues. I focus on healing myself first and then into healing with you and others as I try to wrap my mind around all these changes and mistakes I've made in the past—surrendering to them and not judging myself for them. Remember the failures and let them serve as a reminder but don't let them control me or the self-image I have of myself.

That becomes the lesson today, nothing more. Stay curious, love yourself, be a loving presence for others. Do that and you'll stay on the right path in life, in your passions, and in love.

DAY 11

The Tipping Point

"I FALL IN LOVE EVERY DAY. NOT WITH PEOPLE, BUT WITH SITUATIONS."
—AMY WINEHOUSE, MUSICIAN

Lesson Learned – You can wish and wish for something to happen, but in the end, if it's meant to be it will work out, and if it's not it won't. That shit is easy as hell to type; it's hard as hell to live.

Highest High – I made love with someone for the first time in my life on August 19, 2020.

Owen,

Today was a rollercoaster of emotions. Today was challenging. Today was amazing.

Danielle texted me around 10 a.m. in response to a couple messages I had sent the night before on social media. I was essentially just sharing my thoughts of how this could play out once we were able to have a conversation about all of this. How I've changed and what that could look like moving forward if she were open to it. She was open to that and heard my messages, thanked me, and that was pretty much that last night.

But today after sleeping on it, she let me know she didn't see that happening again between us as it would be too painful. Too much damage had been done. I was crushed, obviously.

65

I simply replied that I have so much to say and show her and pleaded her to give me that opportunity at least. She agreed to meet me today at 3:30 p.m. Damn.

Where do I even begin with her? What do I say?

I decided I'd look through a list I had made and pick out the two or three things that were most powerful for me. They explained my past behaviors and then also what has changed. I'd then let the conversation go from there. She and I have always been good about listening and thoughtfully responding to each other. Let's see how this works.

3:30 p.m. rolls around, and it was a long four hours. Time is still relative.

I'll never forget the next six or so hours for the rest of my life. She walked in, and I was changing in the back room, my bedroom. She walked up to me and said simply, "Hey."

I respond with a gentle, "Hello." I'm like a wobbly baby deer trying to stand up at this point. She wraps her arms around me and gives me the biggest hug I've ever had in my life. Neither of us says a word for five minutes. We both just cry.

About five minutes in, I mustered the energy to say, "I'm sorry," as we both kept crying, hugging, and not speaking. A few more minutes pass and I thank her for saving my life through tears still rolling down my face. We eventually lay down on the bed to keep talking and holding each other.

She didn't have much to say nor should she. I even asked her at one point if she wanted to say anything, and she simply replied, "I don't have much to say, but I'll listen."

I grabbed her hand and said, "Let me show you something." I began to show her the main points of my growth to this point. The fact that I haven't been in or seen a healthy relationship in 39 years and how alcohol had made me a shell of myself mentally and physically (just like she had been telling me). It had ruined my emotions and my ability to process those emotions. That obviously makes loving someone extremely difficult and unhealthy for everyone involved.

I talked briefly about all that I've learned touching on all the things I wrote to you about. The conversation lasts maybe five minutes. She says five words, mostly nodding.

Then something incredible happened. We lay back down, cried, and held each other some more. Before either of us knew it we naturally, organically, and effortlessly ended up kissing, touching, and feeling each other in a way I've never experienced before—not only the physical part but more importantly the emotional part.

My heart was full—full of joy and full of love. It was one of the most amazing experiences of my life.

I'm 39 years old, and I don't recall having made love before, not like that. I've had partners; I've had sex (obviously, you exist) but mostly with alcohol involved in some way and never with this type of mental, physical, and emotional connection. Sex when sober is much better.

Sex with an incredibly powerful, heartfelt, passionate, physical, and emotional connection—that's not possible intoxicated. You can't feel it all. You can't experience it. Your senses are numbed; it's not the same. I see that now; I feel that now.

And it's been amazing to be able to experience all of this with Danielle when I was worried that I'd never be able to kiss her again, touch her skin, and hear and feel her in person.

It all happened so quickly, so passionately, that I was almost late to teach my back-to-back yoga classes that night starting at 5:30 p.m. Danielle and I knew there were still things to say since we didn't talk much before, and so we agreed to see each other again before we went to bed and to not spend the night together no matter how much we wanted to. We still needed space.

My two classes flew by. They went well but went quickly. My mind raced. We met back at my place around 9 p.m. and spent the next two hours continuing to alternate between the best sex of my life and tears of love and sadness. Touching, kissing, going places we'd never been before physically and emotionally. Where had this been before? Where had I been before? Our sex and chemistry were always great but not like this. This is unbelievable.

She left a little before 11 p.m., and we were both equally worn out, extremely satisfied, and curious to see what tomorrow would hold for us. I look forward to it with a joy and curiosity that I haven't felt in years. Honestly, I can't even remember the last time I felt like this.

I'm reminded by these feelings, these emotions, of what puppy love feels like. The first time in middle school when you find someone you really care about, when you think you have the world figured out, and you swear you've met your Juliet or Romeo.

Then you'll break up a month later. You'll be heartbroken, and you'll swear you'll never find another girl like her, but then you will. That's love at the early stages. It goes on like that for years.

In high school, you become a little less emotional about it but not much. The love and relationships intensify and lengthen. You explore things sexually too, which deepens the feelings, the connection.

Eventually, you get to college, like I did with Cassie, where you find a girl you actually think you could marry. Cassie was the first girl I felt like that about. She was 5'10 or so, pretty and dark-haired, which I always fell for; she had an athletic body and amazing ass.

Our sex was really good too. I learned in relationships, especially the physical part, that you get out of them what you put into them. That's often where most guys fail. They get theirs, and they don't care about the women. Don't be like that. Take care of your women, and in return they will take care of you.

With Cassie, our relationship was one of love and basketball like the movie. We'd shoot baskets together late at night, talk about our frustrating performances, and laugh about our good ones. We could relate to the successes of being the best player on the team and the pressures that come along with that.

Her teams were always better than mine. The girls teams at my university were always really good. We were usually around .500. I'll always remember Cassie, though, like I will Danielle because you don't forget the girls that you love, physically and emotionally. The ones that truly move you, that truly impact you.

I messed it up with Cassie, eventually. A relationship that started off not exactly on the up and up would end that way too. There were too many blurred lines of what was healthy between us and what wasn't. Are we together this month or not? It was messy in the end.

But she'll always hold a place in my heart. They always do. I share this with you now because I don't know what will happen with Danielle. We may end up like Cassie and I did, unable to ever get on the same page with what the relationship is and what we want it to eventually become. Finding the same mindset, love, and respect for each other in a healthy way that allows growth will be tough. You have to combine all three to make love work.

All three of these won't always align. There can be ebbs and flows in this just like with everything we have discussed so far. Life is always about that balance, the middle path. Relationships long for the right path too.

Practice patience, practice love, and practice empathy. Start there, and you're on your way. You're all of three years old right now so you have some time, but it will be here before you know it. I hope you enjoy and stay present in each and every one of those relationships.

DAY 12

The High

Lesson Learned – Love is the trickiest of all human emotions—the most powerful and the most intoxicating. The easiest to feel and the most difficult to understand. Once you find it, find it in a healthy way. You want so badly to hold it and control it, and that's the very way you kill it. Enjoy it, be present with it, nourish it then let it flow naturally. That's the way it stays with you and your partner.

Highest High – Touching again. Kissing again. Seeing a loving smile. Feeling. Hearing a joy-filled laugh and gazing into beautiful eyes—all the things I thought I'd never do again.

Owen,

As I reflect back on last night into today, I continue to be astonished at what felt like one of the best experiences of my life with Danielle. We both woke up texting each other today about the emotion-filled experience.

She was very complimentary about this different Ryan and said that she didn't want to hear promises of how I changed or what I'll do differently but simply continue to show her. I think that's incredibly smart and thoughtful.

We also are both aware that this is now a long game, one day at a time and all, but if this is going to work for us both we have so much growing and healing to still do personally. That's not even taking into consideration our families and those conversations that will eventually need to take place. However, worrying about any of that now is unhealthy—wasted energy.

For now, it's continuing to live in the moment and enjoying each other's company, each other's growth, and each other's passionate love.

I go meet with my therapist at 3 p.m. Holy shit, what a difference a week makes. She, like Danielle, comments on how different I look and sound. How after just seven days she can see and hear the difference in me. That felt great.

We can't see ourselves in the lows or the highs. We're too caught up in our own picture. It helps to be acknowledged, to hear these healthy decisions and actions are noticeable not only within me but to others as well.

I then head to a meeting with the group that I first met with last Thursday. It's a good group of guys that mean well, but they are really rigid, even negative, in their understanding of recovery. I know some people need that, but it hasn't sat really well for me so far.

There is a Buddhist 12-step program at the temple you and I go to, which I think will be fun to explore. I bought the book they use called *One Breath at a Time* today. I'm excited to start to dive into that later tonight and tomorrow.

Danielle and I meet back at my apartment. What would follow was more of the beautiful passionate lovemaking that ensued the night before—bodies shaking and pulsating, kissing and touching, looking into each other's eyes deeply in a way we had never done before, and going to a place we'd never been before.

The lovemaking lasted for two hours that equally seemed to fly by and last forever—a balance that may seem difficult to understand but makes total sense when you're in the moment.

We talk and make love with the candles burning and a playlist of some of our favorites. The soft-spoken vibes of Ray LaMontagne, Trevor Hall, John Mayer, and Amos Lee fill the room. Soft guitar melodies and songs of love lost and gained—all the emotions we've felt over the past few weeks and feel now more than ever.

This was another one of the most beautiful days of my life—healing, impactful, thoughtful, and sexual for both Danielle and I. It was a truly beautiful experience.

I continue to share these stories with you knowing you won't read this until it's age appropriate but also because I want you to know and understand the importance of a genuine and sober love. I thought I had to be intoxicated before to enjoy the company of a beautiful female and to enjoy our sexual experience, but that's not the case.

We think drugs and alcohol heighten our experience, and to be totally honest they can, on occasion. But just like with anything in life, from sex to sports, there are no highs without lows. Anything we become dependent on, that heightens our experience, whether it be physically with a partner or physically as an athlete, there's eventually a low.

For every swing of the pendulum in one direction there's a swing back. That swing takes us lower, and you feel worse. That's why it's necessary to try and do the important things in life as sober as we can.

That way we accurately judge the impact it's having on us, how it feels, and changes we need to make. When we have these important decisions to make in life as partners or professionally as athletes (whatever the case may be), the more often we can make these decisions clear-headed, honestly, and truthfully the better off we'll be in our performance and in our decision-making.

I had three major decision making points in my athletic career as a player and coach. Those were really heavy moments or decisions that would impact my career. I remember them all so vividly; it's incredible. The first was totally sober and may not have been as much of a choice as it was a realization.

It was back during my senior year of high school at another holiday tournament. This time in Coffeyville, Kansas—a booming metropolis if there ever was one. They had a pretty talented tournament though, and you could argue that I was the best player in it—one of the best two or three for sure.

The tournament was also crucial for me because college coaches want to see you compete against the best. This tournament had some good talent, some teams from the inner city, and then another talented team from the outskirts of Kansas City known as Leavenworth High School. I had put myself on the map against them by playing really well in one of my first varsity tournaments by shutting down a senior player on their team that was getting D1 looks.

I remember a D1 coach leaving and saying, "If this sophomore can shut him down then why should we recruit him and not just recruit the sophomore?" That made me feel really good.

Fast forward two years and I had some high Division I schools in attendance to watch me play, from BCS level high majors to schools like the University of San Diego, which was one of the schools I wanted to attend that was actively recruiting me.

I'll never forget the first play of the game. We ran a play where I put my fist up and everyone flattened out. I'd just go one on one against my defender and usually score or get a good shot. Everyone we had played to that point would stay next to their man when I called the play.

On this night, the guys guarding our shooters in the corner didn't stay with them. They stayed at the elbows of the free throw lane. I would now be going 1 on 3 if I tried to score. Leavenworth had scouted us exceptionally well, and I was in trouble.

I'd finish with eight points and foul out with six minutes to go. It was the worst game, easily, of my senior year in high school. None of the scouts even acknowledged me after the game.

My mom and dad had come to visit me in the hotel lobby, and I remember sitting in some shitty hotel recliner. I felt like I had the weight of the world on my shoulders. I knew the D1 hopes had pretty much gone down with that performance. That was going to be my last chance to really impress, barring a state championship type run, which wouldn't happen.

My mom and dad tried to remain relatively positive, but they knew I didn't want to hear it. I never liked fake conversation even in high school. They knew that.

"Looks like juco for me," I'd eventually mumble. Knowing that if I still wanted to hold on to my Division I dreams (which are stupid by the way as lots of Division II schools are way better than Division I schools both athletically and academically), I'd have to go to a junior college and prove I could play at that level.

The weight, though, at that moment when you realize something you've worked for, something so important to you all falls down with one bad performance is heavy. I can't even imagine having something like that happen on a championship or Olympic level. I now understood why so many of them struggle with the mental side of their lives. It gets back to those waves and those pendulum swings—always highs and lows, never balanced, and never mindful.

Ultimately, all you can do is get back up, play the next game, and show up at the next practice—just like in life.

The sun came up the next day. Everyone went on living their lives. I continued my athletic career—a successful one.

The reality is those moments don't define us. Our lives are a series of moments, all affecting each other, yet independent of each other. However, not all my stories as an athlete are happy and not all my stories of drinking and partying are destructive and negative. Most importantly, they've all made me exactly who I am today—a person I now love, appreciate, and am excited to see and spend time with again. For that, I'm grateful.

Week 3

Grow

DAY 13

A Difficult Fate

Lesson Learned – I realize today that I still have a lot of healing to do. This realization occurs after Danielle and I take a step back, which illuminates how much I still need to repair and grow.

Lowest Low – I felt a withdrawal today, physically. Not one that was craving alcohol, but one that was craving something else physically and intensely. I think my body is still cleaning itself up.

I filled it with sugar, which is a healthier solution than alcohol, but not one that will last long term. I have Owen today though and his presence, his love makes me grateful. It brings me peace mentally and physically.

Owen,

Friday was one of the tougher days, not surprisingly, after spending the last day and a half with Danielle. It brings to light how much work I still have to do.

While the relationship with Danielle is infinitely healthier and happier, human nature is making it difficult now to go without her and focus back on my growth and healing. Instead, I think of when I can feel all those intense and powerful emotions that Danielle and I felt the last two nights. It is a challenge. I also know it's what I should be doing.

You help a ton although you've been a bit emotional today. That tends to be the case when you spend more time with your mom, like you have the last few days, even though it is supposed to be a 50/50 split. I think that's a good thing though. You get your mom's energy, positivity, and emotional tendencies. You get my calm demeanor, focus and drive, and my mindful makeup.

I found myself having to pump sugar into my body due to the withdrawals from Danielle and you being emotional. I had been trying to cut back on carbs and sugar to lean up a little bit. Instead, I had a couple Sprites today, some Starburst, and a bunch of fruit. It calmed the uneasiness, which is key, but the sugar need was real today.

My body again has an intense need for work. I have too much energy mentally and physically to finish the day without doing something active. There's a new type of fire in my life, which is good. It makes me sharper, and I get more done during the day. Before, I was lucky to work two or three hours in a day. I now work seven or eight easily and still have energy for you and a workout.

Overall, I know I'm in a much better space two weeks in. The waves come a lot less often, and they are a lot less intense. I'm more productive with work and with my mental and physical well-being. I'm better.

If today has taught me anything it's that there is a long way to go in terms of more reading, more journaling, more healing, a deeper dive into the past, and understanding how that affects the present.

Those two paths are always intertwined, the past and the present, or what we may perceive as good or bad. Some people call it fate; I don't believe in fate. I think we make our own path and that things happen for a reason although we may not understand them at the time.

Take that fateful night in Coffeyville that I talked about yesterday—the night my Division I chances took a hit. The biggest school I had talking to me in any capacity was Oklahoma State. They had a really good point guard in Doug Gottlieb but still needed someone to back him up in what would amount to very limited minutes, most likely even a red-shirt year.

I didn't go after that Coffeyville performance, and they were also boosted by the transfer of another high-level point guard in Victor Williams—an all-conference type of point guard in the Big 12. There was no longer a place for me on the team especially after playing poorly.

If I would have gone to Oklahoma State, even in year two, I'd have barely played or been a red-shirt type of player—one that wouldn't have traveled, most likely, with the rest of the team on the main plane. I'd have traveled in the second plane with personnel like the basketball ops team or the radio crew.

On January 27, 2001, the plane carrying two of the walk-on type of players, their radio crew, and basketball operations team crashed killing all 10 passengers on board. Would I have been on that plane if I went to Oklahoma State? Maybe or maybe not. The point is we can let our mind run crazy thinking about a million what-ifs in life wondering about our fate.

We can question decisions we make, sure. But instead, I'd like you to think of all the times you've avoided a room or party because something feels off, you've ignored or ghosted someone you barely knew because something about them just doesn't feel right. There are times we don't realize our intuition, our unconscious mind is telling us what to do.

Carl Jung, the early 1900s psychiatrist, has a great quote on this. He says, "Until we make the unconscious conscious it will direct our lives and we will call it fate." This is another example of saying there is no such thing as fate, and that we have the control. I totally agree.

We can say all these random events or decisions in our lives were lucky or unlucky. That something was predetermined, destined to happen, but that's not reality. Something happens; we choose our reaction.

Once we get a result we can choose to dwell on that result, make excuses if it's bad, talk about what should have or could have happened, how our lives would be different. Or we can accept what happened in our lives with grace and understand that what happened to us may have instead happened for us.

That subtle shift makes all the difference in the world, Ower you go from thinking about what happens for you in your life vers happens to you and shift from a fate or luck mindset to one where you control your destiny.

I could have spun a million butterfly effects into how my college career played out or how my coaching career played out. But the reality is I believe all these things that happen for us in our lives are meant to change us, shape us, and mold us and our existence into exactly what it was meant to be.

If I, at the age of 39, didn't have this series of circumstances unfold exactly how they have, I wouldn't be writing this book right now. If I didn't play that bad game that night, and then decide not to go to junior college, or to Oklahoma State, or whatever other random shift in the universe we could discuss then I wouldn't be right here, right now writing this book.

And that's exactly where I'm supposed to be. You are exactly where you are supposed to be. That's the beauty of life and perhaps, equally importantly, the beauty of mindfulness. You are on your right path. Enjoy the journey.

Remain present in your life personally, professionally, and athletically. Surround yourself with people that will attract positive things, have positive ideals, and then understand what happens as a result of that is not fate. It's quite the opposite actually. It's you working, attracting, and then deserving the things that happen to you in your life.

I see that now more clearly than ever. These past couple years have been immensely challenging for me in every area of my life. But I wouldn't change a thing. I finally know and feel that I'm doing exactly what I'm meant to be doing.

I'm helping athletes and coaches find mindfulness, meditation, sport-specific yoga, and mental health in their careers. I'm a great father. I'm a successful writer and mental skills coach. I work with professional athletes and coaches that others would dream of working with. I don't say this to brag, but I say this because none of this would have happened for me if I didn't go through every single experience I have gone through in my life.

That's not fate. That's my path; that's my journey.

DAY 14

Emotional Dragons

"WE FORGE THE CHAINS WE WEAR IN LIFE."
—CHARLES DICKENS, WRITER

Lesson Learned – Balancing health, growth, and repair will be extremely difficult over the next few weeks and months.

Highest High – It's difficult processing these confusing emotions sober and trying to heal a relationship. I feel like I'm making it worse for Danielle at times and more difficult for me in the process even though I want so badly for it to work.

Owen,

Today was the first full Saturday I've had you since my sobriety. You've been great, and it's amazing how the touch or kind words from an almost four-year-old can penetrate so deep and be so healing.

At times, when I'm getting frustrated and feeling my emotions start to boil, you'll gently touch my hand and calm me down. At night, we'll be lying in bed, and you'll pat me on my back and tell me how much you love me. It's so impressive for someone as young as you to possess such genuine love, such pure kindness. You're amazing. You've been a calming influence throughout these past two weeks.

We've had a busy schedule, which has been helpful, and it's what most people prefer. "An idle mind is the devil's workshop."

But I've learned that the opposite is true. An idle mind, a quiet mind is actually a great way to live. Being calm and comfortable in silence makes for the happiest and healthiest life. The masses are taught to stay busy and keep their hands busy. Don't think too much. Don't listen to your mind or your body.

As I look back on those types of thoughts and belief systems, I find them comical. I know a lot of those beliefs originate from the athletic world where they want us all to be robots that are used for their physical abilities only. "Don't talk about your emotions. Don't talk about any pain you might be feeling physically and emotionally. Just go out there, perform, and shut up."

"Do your job as an athlete and don't say anything" is one of the unhealthiest mantras that exist. I'm starting to see how that trickled into my personal life. Part of what made alcohol attractive to me was that alcohol numbed everything, good and bad, and it was always there for me.

Alcohol became a good friend and saying goodbye to that friend that helped me so much through the years when I was going through some of these things physically and emotionally was really tough. I was breaking up with a partner of over 20 years.

But we had an abusive relationship. That's the part I didn't realize. Reading and going to meetings has helped me to see that. The way it made me feel and think was dark as fuck. I hated who I was, who I became, and that was all because of alcohol. Yet I couldn't let it go because I was so isolated in the end that I thought it was one of my only friends especially when Danielle and I were off.

I see how distorted my reality had become and that alcohol isolates you purposefully like that. It kills your brain, kills your emotions, and the ability to process those emotions. That's why I said it was never my friend; it was my worst enemy. It's like a bizarre Stockholm syndrome.

That's probably the best way I can describe it. I fell in love with my captor in a way I never thought possible even though I knew all these shitty things it was making me do and feel. As I mentioned earlier, I felt like Frodo, and it had become my precious.

Like in *Lord of the Rings* with Frodo, in order for anything to become that powerful it has to initially form a bond in what appears to be a healthy and happy way. Alcohol did that for me early on.

There were so many nights where a girl would come up to me at a nightclub or bar knowing who I was because I played basketball at a Division II school 30 minutes away from my hometown. My jersey was retired from my high school. You can walk in there to this day and see my picture and my jersey number hanging up in the gym.

Take that fame, that notoriety, and mix in some alcohol along with some late 90s R & B and you have a concoction that will lead to some fun and memorable nights. I had many.

A specific example of a typical Saturday while I was in college, in season? We'd have a game that night, usually around 7. The result didn't matter. We were going out. We'd start drinking in our apartment even though at my school it was a dry campus, and then one of us would make sure we were sober enough to drive us all to the club.

This particular night my roommate, his name is DJ, and I were dating freshman best friends. We were juniors I think. We all four went to the club together with our other roommate, JB. Five of us deep in an SUV, drinking to the sound of loud music, all laughs and smiles, and without a care in the world.

There was a window, while I was in college, where this one nightclub ran the entire city of Springfield. It was called Remingtons. Everyone went there on Saturday nights, and Springfield is a college town with our Division II rival, Drury, and then a Division I school, Missouri State. When I say everyone I mean it. It was a literal perfect storm with nowhere else people went in Springfield on Saturday nights. Everyone was there.

That meant three universities worth of women, three universities worth of athletes, and long island iced teas that cost $1. There was a huge dance floor, beautiful women, loud music, cheap drinks, and good times. Plenty of hookups would occur on a given night and usually a fight, or two, as well.

We'd always go to my childhood house after the club when my mother was out of town. It was right down the street, a giant house with four bedrooms, where we could be as loud as we wanted. On this particular night, we already had two beautiful women with us. DJ and I were all set. JB would end up smoking weed on the couch playing Tiger Woods golf on the PlayStation 2.

I remember vividly that there was a moment on this night when I had already gone up to the bedroom and had sex with the beautiful woman. It was now around 3 a.m. I was drunk off of alcohol, a little high off of weed although I was never a big smoker, and sitting there on this nice leather couch playing Tiger Woods gold with JB.

This beautiful girl walks out in her lingerie—phenomenal body, beautiful face, great ass, and she's asking me to come back to bed so we can sleep. Here I am, the starting point guard and best player on my college basketball team, one of the best players in our entire conference, drunk and slightly high. I played a great game hours before, and now this beautiful girl is asking me to come to bed at 3 a.m. We'd most likely have sex again before we went to bed and then again in the morning when we woke up.

That's just one night, but a variation of that night happened hundreds of times with dozens of women over the next 15 years as an athlete and coach. You can see how that lifestyle would be intoxicating. You can see how that lifestyle would even become addicting.

Beautiful women, cheap drinks, loud music, and a good looking face that these beautiful women almost always recognized. All I had to do was grab a drink, slide up to them, and "Ask you what your interests are, who you be with, things to make you smile, what numbers to dial?" Kidding, that's a line from one of the best rappers of all time, Notorious B.I.G. You'll learn about him later in life. But you get the point. It was incredibly fun and relatively easy—not the women but the process. I was set up to succeed.

I'm not telling you to not experience that. In fact, quite the opposite. Everyone should experience that lifestyle if they can in a safe and respectful way especially toward the women you are with when you go out. Even more so if you are lucky enough to take them home at the end of the night.

But you can also see how that becomes a slow descent into a dangerous pit that you can't escape from, an athletic quicksand. You start chasing an alcohol-infused female dragon that will never fulfill you like you desire when the alcohol and drugs are involved to that extent.

It becomes a balance. You want to avoid that all powerful ring around your neck that starts out as something light and fun and then becomes a powerful and controlling force that dictates your life. It took 19 years for that to happen to me. It took 19 years for me to throw that ring into the volcano.

There will be plenty of fun nights like the one I just described. Just make sure you are drinking or smoking to heighten them and not because you can't function or have fun without them.

DAY 15

Chop Wood; Carry Water

Lesson Learned – At a meeting today, I learned that sometimes the person in recovery can heal much quicker than those around them. Some of the people we hurt need more time than we do to heal wounds, process emotions, and see if love is still in their hearts for us.

Lowest Low – Trying to navigate sober difficult emotions especially when I'm trying to do good and be good. It's much harder to process these raw emotions and failures when you are genuinely trying and it's still not good enough. That's tough.

Owen,

I experienced some great growth today. It all started with me fucking up last night. I sent Danielle an emotionally triggering video of you. I was only trying to help as she had been asking about you, but I'm learning now that's not what matters. Intent isn't always forgivable like that; there's a balance in knowing what you should and shouldn't do, what's appropriate and what's too soon.

Don't get me wrong. Intent does matter in the messages we send and how we communicate them. You can't and shouldn't intentionally be an asshole. But as I learned in my communication and empathic listening training, the impact lies in how the receiver then receives the message. And, in this case, she found it to be fucked up. The delivery and message were both not helpful for her. In fact, they were the opposite.

This is where the growth took place for me. A realization to be more thoughtful in my messaging, my tone, and the vulnerability of something as intimate as a video of you.

The other part of the equation, however, is if both sides are trying with good, thoughtful, and empathic intentions, and it's still broken then you may have a problem. Both people can mean well, and it's simply not meant to be. It's not a good match.

It was a bizarre day for me emotionally as Danielle was doing one of the most powerful and incredible things she's done since I've known her. She went skydiving for the first time ever.

Obviously, there's a risk involved in that, and I wanted to say how much I loved her before she went, but she wasn't in a great space. I texted her anyway and said I loved her. Then I didn't hear from her for several hours.

Around 7:30 p.m. I heard back, and she was still noticeably upset. She called and raised her voice. I don't think she meant it in an aggressive way, but one that was simply upset and agitated at our conversation the night before.

Here's where the growth took place.

I didn't try and excuse the behavior or be manipulative like I normally would have in the past. I listened. She talked about how my texts and the video I sent of you were emotionally triggering for her and said that she'll see and speak to you when she's ready and healed emotionally. It's not for me to decide.

I listened. I understood.

Danielle did allow me to communicate how I thought she was missing you due to comments over the past week. Obviously, I didn't send them to intentionally trigger her, but I also took accountability in that I misunderstood the intent of her comments. I should have asked her first if she would have liked me to send a video of you that may have been emotionally triggering for her. This is where the growth started to take place.

Instead of trying to argue with Danielle and make her see my point of view and how I was trying to help her, shift her into a box to fit my narrative, I empathetically listened. I heard what she was trying to tell me and how it made her feel and think about the situation. I listened, I took it in, and I learned.

What happened as a result?

When Danielle angrily started the conversation she also said, "I'd be over there right now if it weren't for those text messages and you sending them to play with my emotions."

I knew she wanted to spend time with me. I heard her, I felt her, and we truly communicated. It's extremely difficult, but I feel like we are making progress together.

In life, I've learned that we don't end up making these drastic changes overnight. It's a slow and methodical process. "Chop wood; carry water," as the Zen proverb goes.

Repetition.

If you want to be good at anything, you have to rep the hell out of it with intentionality. You have to want to improve and strive to make those improvements daily—in slow, oftentimes, painful ways. This is true of love. This is true of life, and this is true in sports.

I wasn't used to sitting uncomfortably in conversation with Danielle especially when I didn't agree with what she was saying when I was trying to be helpful for her. I didn't like sitting in that uncomfortable space not only now but for what I knew was going to be days and weeks.

I also didn't like it when going into my junior year of college the university I was playing at recruited a junior college point guard. There's only one reason your school recruits a junior college point guard when they already have a junior point guard on the team.

They don't think you're good enough. They want to make it an open competition. That made me uncomfortable.

The good news was I had an entire summer now to prepare for this new competition. The point guard they brought in was the antithesis of me. I was 6'3, long and an above average athlete even for basketball standards. But I was not quick. I controlled tempo, saw the floor incredibly well, played hard, and shot the ball from deep just OK.

My competition was 5'8 on a good day, lightning quick, shot it well, was really strong, and had a good enough handle with the ball that he could break people down off the bounce.

They had clearly brought in someone to do the things they thought I could not do.

I busted my ass that summer. I beefed up to 192 pounds of healthy, strong weight. I got thousands of shots up and played a ton of pick-up that included a pro-am league that was really high-level in my hometown of Springfield. Several professional basketball players that were playing overseas would come home to Springfield and play in the league over the summer.

Repetition. That's what I did. I got up a ton of shots. I practiced guarding similar players in the pro-am league that I would be seeing with my internal competition next season. I went into that year as good a player as I had ever been in my career. I was ready.

What would unfold was exactly what I had hoped, what I had planned for, and what I was intentional about. The repetitions paid off. In the first game of the season versus a Division I opponent in Western Illinois, I had 13 assists in a single game and never looked back.

Over the course of the year, I'd have two triple doubles in one year from the point guard spot, a feat that wouldn't be repeated in the entire conference for almost 20 years and still hasn't happened at the school since.

I shot the ball well from outside, for me anyway. I was physical, strong, took care of the ball, and would finish in the top five in steals in the entire country and top 20 in assists. I had one of the best statistical point guard seasons in school history. Most of the records I'd set that year still stand today.

The irony is not lost on me as I reflect back on this year for me as an athlete, and this day for me years later doing repetitions outside your comfort zone. Find something that you value enough and do things you've never done before in order to achieve whatever it is you are trying to achieve.

Relationship-wise, it was living in the uncomfortable space with Danielle. Getting repetitions of those difficult conversations, sitting in the awkward space sober, and being OK with it. Trying to learn, sit in discomfort, and become a better partner as a result.

The same was true of my junior year of college as an athlete. I had to sit in the uncomfortable space of knowing they had just recruited another point guard to take my spot or at least challenge me for it.

I sat in discomfort and then made the conscious decision to let that discomfort turn me into a better player. I had the best season of my athletic career as a result.

In life, for meaningful growth to occur, we also must experience that discomfort and sit with it. Generate intentional repetitions of the necessary changes that will make you better. Sit in discomfort until those changes occur. Then experience the beauty and success of those changes, of that growth.

DAY 16

Halfway to Forever

Lesson Learned – Patience, gratitude, understanding, and communication are all really tricky to do regularly and in a way that's genuine. But once you start to understand what they really mean, the sky is the fucking limit (another Biggie reference!) with your growth and with your relationships.

Lowest Low – Balancing growth and self-love with a program that seemingly tries to keep you reminded of your lows in life.

Owen,

Halfway to 30 days today. They tell us in meetings to not think of it that way, one day at a time. "Just don't drink today." I can't help but think about 30 days and larger numbers. My mind operates differently than most in this process. Even my sister, Nikki, who has been incredible throughout has started to question at least to some degree my sobriety and my approach to it.

Don't get me wrong. I trust her and her husband, Jim, completely, but it feels as though my mind and behaviors work differently than theirs. I see now why the AA system works so well for them. They thrive on the structure, the rigidity, the no wiggle room of AA.

You are a drunk; you will always be an alcoholic. There is no cure or answer in being a drunk. Stick with the program.

Nikki even sent me a page tonight from a chapter I had already read that uses words like we are delusional if we think we can stop. We will never regain control; we will constantly get worse not better. We've lost our legs, and no kind of treatment can help us with the problem of drinking.

All that may be true and is true to them, but to be constantly bashed over the head with these negative reminders in a constant negative barrage of language has been hard to read. The message is hard to accept, at least for me, at least to this point.

As I mentioned, I have started the Buddhist version of 12 steps, and that reading is much more aligned with my thinking. Perhaps therein lies the answer in what I need to do, and how I need to approach everything. I'm supposed to have a meeting with a spiritual advisor, Victor, on Thursday, but I need to push that back so that I can practice and meet with Susan.

I think that's where a bit of the confusion lies with my sister, at least from her perspective. I put in around 40 hours' worth of work these past two weeks on just myself and my healing.

I write, I read, I journal, and I go to therapy. I talk about my emotions, both past and present. It's been extremely challenging. Probably the hardest thing I've ever done. And I know I'm just getting started.

But I am doing the work. I am trying to the best of my awareness. And I think I'm doing great, but who the hell knows?

All I can do at this point is to continue to be compassionate to myself and those around me. Practice that self-love and acceptance that was so powerful for me in the beginning of all of this. With that patience, growth and grace, I'll end up where I'm meant to be doing the things I was meant to do all so I can impact the athletic world.

That will all happen. I know it in my heart. And I truly believe you were born to me to help me be a part of it. I don't say that as pressure. I say it as you are creating a ripple, a shift in my path.

But for now, it's still head down so that I can get healthy and gain clarity on what all of this looks and feels like emotionally, personally, and then, finally, professionally.

Finding your purpose in life, what you're supposed to do, is heavy to think about just like with sobriety. I choose not to think in lengths of time but to remain present and focus on staying on the right path.

Finding that path is difficult. There aren't giant flashing neon signs that say, "Go this way." We never know where our path is going and if it's the right path or not. Like I mentioned a few days ago, each decision has a ripple effect in our lives that I think leads us to exactly where we are supposed to be.

As I left college, I had another one of those life-altering decisions.

I finished up another disappointing senior season as a team. We took a step back as a program. By the end of the year, we were down four of our projected starters. I was all that was left. I led the team in points, assists, steals, rebounds, and turnovers. That's not something that should happen at the Division II level—one person leading in all those categories.

It illustrates the lack of help I had that year. It also put me in a position to explore playing professionally, overseas.

I had an opposing coach from the conference connect me to an agent from Iowa. I'd have a tryout with several other all-conference players from different conferences around the Midwest. I needed to prep first.

I busted my ass again, got in great shape, and did lots of repetitions like we discussed. I was ready and was going to play one more pick-up game before I left. A bunch of current D1 players and pros were back for the summer. There were some really high-level games.

In the last game of the night, a 6'8, 250-pound mountain of a man went up for a rebound and pulled it down violently. I would always slap up at the ball when a big man brought down a rebound to see if I could sneak in and get a steal. It didn't work.

Instead, what resulted was an elbow directly to my bicep. It was so severe the doctors thought for a moment they'd have to cut my arm open to drain blood as I was starting to lose feeling in my fingers. I missed the tryout.

I got another chance months later—a second chance right before the overseas season began. Their seasons usually start in September. I ramped up my training again and headed up to Iowa. I played well.

Another player from my conference, Larry Taylor, also made second-team all-MIAA with me. He was there too and played well. He was an athletic combo type guard and was good. There was a team looking for two guards in Brazil, and they'd start us at $10,000 and expenses for the year. Go over there and get hurt, and you'd get cut. If you had a couple bad weeks, you'd be cut. It was cutthroat over there, obviously.

This was a beginner type league that paid like shit but was a start. It was common for D2 players like him and me especially players that weren't big scorers. We had a decision to make—take the job, take the money, and build a risky pro career or start our nonathlete lives. He played, and I hung them up.

I instead took a junior college coaching job for $12,000 and room and board at Eastern Arizona College, a junior college in Thatcher, Arizona. The room and board position wasn't that of a resident director or anything like that. I lived in the dorms like a student would. But it was a start like Larry had in Brazil.

Why'd I take the job then? Why not just live in Brazil and try it out? I was tired of the grind. I was tired of being hurt. I was tired of losing. I was tired of the unknown. I was tired of it all. I needed something different. A different challenge in life, hopefully something healthier for me mentally and physically.

Larry quickly moved up the ranks in Brazil. By the end of his career, he was making significant six figures in the leagues he played in. He got his Brazilian citizenship, and he even played in the Olympics for Brazil in 2012. It was an incredible story. He played against the likes of Kobe Bryant, LeBron James, Kevin Durant, James Harden, and so on. I remember watching the game on TV. I was genuinely proud of him. He had made it.

I don't regret my decision, once again. I had played too hard, and my body was worn down. I did think about my career and how it would have been different with better teammates. I'd have to do less and could have extended my career. Perhaps, with better trainers or medical staff they could have cleaned some things up on my body that would have made me a step quicker and more athletic.

Or, as I mentioned with Oklahoma State, maybe the opposite happens. Time spent on the past is time wasted, or life can be filled with what ifs. I choose to stay in the present and enjoy the journey I'm on.

There's an irony in today, halfway to what felt like forever of the first 30 days of sobriety for me. I'm also about to turn 40 in January 2021. Another halfway type point, but this time on a larger scale.

I love where I'm headed on this journey. It's nice to step back at this halfway point and simply observe where I've been, where I'm headed, but most importantly, where I am now.

DAY 17

Another Level

Lesson Learned – Balancing health, growth, and repair will be extremely difficult over the next few weeks and months.

Highest High – The connection with Danielle has become so passionate now that in the middle of the day today we couldn't stop texting and telling each other all these super intense emotional and physical desires.

Owen,

The halfway point to forever was also one of the best discussions and healing conversations I've had in a relationship. I feel like I've grown so much and continue to grow.

With each day that passes, I'm reminded of the challenges not only of the day but also of what lies ahead. I also know that any energy spent on what lies ahead is wasted energy. My mantra is, "Stay present, focus on what I can control, and let go of what doesn't serve me."

In the AA program they ask us do the following: "Have the serenity to accept the things we cannot change, the courage to change the things we can, and the wisdom to know the difference." The only thing I'd modify in that would be I think we all need to have the serenity to surrender to the things we cannot change.

Perhaps acceptance fits best for most, but I've found the process to be that of a surrender vs. acceptance. I'm probably splitting hairs there.

In *One Breath at a Time,* the author lists the surrender process as three steps. First, a surrender to the truth of a disease and the inability to control it; then surrendering to a Higher Power seeing that we depend on something besides our own will; and knowledge to stay sober and develop spiritually.

They then go on to say that no one wants to surrender. Therein lies the problem. I felt that way too. That I was too smart and too strong to need help. I could kick it on my own when I wanted to, and it wasn't bad enough yet to need help. All these pieces fall under that unwillingness to surrender. I see that now.

One Breath also talks about how we always want to look up for help. We look to where we want to be, looking up, but that's not where we need to look. That's not what has led us to the problems we currently have, and that most certainly won't help us to recover.

Instead, we must look down into the darkness and shit that lies beneath us. Like the movie *Shawshank Redemption*, we must crawl through that shit to escape. We can't jump the walls; we have to dig our way out slowly and climb through the shit to escape our past, to become free.

One thing I can't free my mind from are my sexual desires and feelings toward Danielle. They are now ramped all the way back up as strong as they have ever been. Luckily, she and I are aware of this and trying to limit the amount of time we are spending with each other.

I think that would surprise most people. If something feels good then do it more often. Spend as much time as you can with that person doing that particular thing. But, not ironically, that just becomes another form of addiction. It's not as lethal and not as unhealthy as say alcohol or drugs, but it's unhealthy nonetheless.

For now, Danielle and I are not spending the night with each other and if we are, we are limiting it to once a week. She's been really good about this part of the relationship, better than me. She's really strong or perhaps more disciplined? I'm not sure how to label this character flaw that I have.

I've noticed this particular character flaw in myself now more than ever. I've always thrown myself into behaviors and activities that I enjoy. I do everything in my life intensely as hell—

everything.

In sports, I wanted to be the best. As a result, I'd play and practice for hours. I'd run sprints until I passed out. I'd shoot baskets outside in the rain and snow. I'd lift weights and complete intense workouts on family vacations in places like San Diego or Hawaii.

I have tremendous drive. I have incredible passion. I compete and push myself in insane ways.

In relationships, I did the same. Let's fast forward into the physically and emotionally intense parts of the relationship. I'd prefer to start having heavy conversations and sex almost immediately with a new partner to try and figure out if things are going to work. I fast forward through the bullshit.

As a result, relationships rarely lasted past three or four months for me. I'd intensely spend time with a new partner until I knew if I wanted the relationship to be long term or not.

About a decade ago, I got into energy drinks. I'd drink three or four 16 oz drinks in a day. I drank so much over a couple years that I started to have heart issues. I had to stop them cold turkey as my heart was about to explode.

Even now, sober, I drink Sprite and eat Starbust, fruit, and other high sugar foods and candies like crazy. It's not uncommon for me to eat a double pack of Starbust in 15 minutes and chase it with a Sprite. Then I won't eat anymore for the rest of the day.

I was like that with alcohol too. It didn't make sense to me to drink unless we were going to get drunk, good and drunk. I started to think about my next beer before I had finished drinking my current one.

I was also competitive in my drinking. If whoever I was with drank 10 beers, I'd drink 11. If they took three shots then I would too.

It's this character flaw for me in life that's also driven me to be really successful. I dive in, all in, be it in my relationships, drinking, athletic career, or coaching career. If I wasn't the best or if it wasn't the best then I usually didn't stay with it for long. I'd move on.

Some would say that's too much, too competitive, but I don't know. I'd be willing to bet anyone that was great at anything had a similar character flaw or trait, which is probably a better way of putting it. Everything in moderation but moderation.

Take my relationship or what exists of it now with Danielle, for example. It's way too soon to start worrying about getting back together and what that will look like for both of us. But that will be a conversation that will come up soon if we continue down this path.

I can't operate in the unknown. Are we moving forward or moving on? Where are we at with all of this? I have no problem being patient, but I need to know we are agreeing to the fact that we are working on things.

The problem is there are so many emotions involved starting with her and me and how we will heal. If we did get back together, she would have some difficult conversations on her side of the family. We've been on and off the last few months of our relationship. The last couple times we stopped talking, we had both pretty well agreed that was it; we were done.

I realize now that was the alcohol talking on my side of things. It had ruined me in so many ways that I was no longer myself. I was always coming down or drinking to get back up, highs and lows. I was never mentally or emotionally there like I should have been. I was living the past few months in handcuffs essentially.

But she was in handcuffs too, and I know her family had to have seen parts of that in her behaviors and personality. And that doesn't even include the shit she talked about me to any of her six sisters.

I tried to keep our relationship to her and I, away from my sisters. And Danielle also saved my life twice. She's got a lot of wiggle room on her end with my family.

On the other hand, I do not. A couple of her sisters had pushed her to move on from me before. We're also 15 years apart in age. I have a son, and I am now in recovery. To an outsider, I can see how that doesn't look great, and to her family that has been witnessing it all first hand, it would look even worse. Danielle has a tendency to talk shit about me too when things are bad. That won't help.

On the positive side, I see how much beauty there is inside of me. I have so much to offer someone with my mind, my love, my sense of humor, my compassion, and my gratitude. I'm a great father and a great lover. I'm smart, funny, empathic, self-aware, and have a healthy meditation and yoga practice.

I'd love nothing more than to give all those gifts to Danielle so that we can grow each other and make each other happier. Our love wouldn't be the reason for our happiness but the final piece of the puzzle in our journey for love, for a fulfilled life.

I know we could do that. However, I do question if we can both see that and figure it out. That's still to be determined.

DAY 18

Life in Transition

Lesson Learned – Combining a Buddhist path on the 12 steps, going to meetings, journaling, and reading have me on my right path. It's a different path, different to what my sister would recommend, but it's the right one for me.

Lowest Low – Transitions in life are really challenging be it from high school to college, college to the real world, or in and out of relationships. They're all extremely difficult to take on and move through successfully. Why don't we ever talk about or teach transitions?

Owen,

Transitions are tough. They take time. They are extremely uncomfortable. We can't prepare for them, and our results are also yet to be determined.

We can't get a feel of how we'll do in our next chapter of life, our next relationship, or whatever it may be.

Those things put together are a terrifying combination for an athlete. In fact, we prepare most of our lives to avoid exactly that. We train, strengthen, control outcomes, scout our opponents, and learn from past mistakes so that we don't repeat them. We hate the unknown.

We can't do any of those things when we transition out of sports and into life.

Transitions are also rarely discussed, rarely taught. There are no classes we take in school. We graduate high school or college, and the world says, "good luck!" as it kicks us out the proverbial door.

No one talks to us about how difficult that process will be, transitioning in and out of the different areas of our lives. From a loving relationship ending in a move across the city or country for a new job to the loss of a loved one or the end of an athletic career, no one tells us what to do, think, or feel. No one tells us how to process these thoughts or emotions. Why is that?

I'm reminded of a book I read last year, *Finding Yourself in Transition* by Robert Brumet. He's a mentor of mine and a spiritual man with a fascinating story.

Robert was a minister in the middle of a difficult divorce and knew he needed something more, something different, to help him. His life was in ruins at the age of 45—divorced and nearly bankrupt. He found mindfulness and meditation. It saved him.

Robert wrote the book about transitions around that time in his life. In turn, it's been very helpful for me during my difficult times. There's a chapter in particular called "The Void" that saved my life in my darkest times.

Just like Robert, I am starting over. I'll be 40 soon but not for a couple months. At least I get a five-year head start.

Robert and I have reconnected as I have gone through all of this. He's helping to mentor me and to see my latest transition in a new light. He helped me to strip everything away, let go of my ego, and focus on the present and what I have in this moment.

We should do this as athletes and coaches too, but no one tells us that.

There's no point in dwelling on past accomplishments or disappointments, worrying about what the future holds, what my next job will be, or who my next partner will be. None of those things are relevant although they feel that way, rather intensely, at the time.

As athletes, we want so badly to control outcomes or feel like we have a lot to do with them. That's our nature. We're conditioned to feel that if we prepare ourselves to the best of our ability and give our best effort then it will work for us. We will do really well.

But life stops working like that once we stop playing or coaching. Granted, from a karma standpoint, we should continue to prepare for a given situation or relationship to the best of our ability. We should give our best effort once we are in our relationship, our job, or a specific situation.

But post athletic career we lose a lot of the power we are accustomed to having. We lose control. That can result in us losing control in our lives too. It did for me.

Robert calls it The Void. It's an empty and dark space in between where you were and where you are going.

Robert says in his book that, "In the Void, time and space seem to lose their reality, self seems like a phantom. The Void touches our deepest fears, and most would do anything to avoid those feelings."

I was doing that, avoiding my feelings with alcohol. It almost broke me physically.

At the beginning of this book, I mentioned my physical break and then my emotional break. It's time to stop breaking and time to start healing. It's time to acknowledge the past and what's been broken, heal that pain, and then release it.

DAY 19

A Reason to Smile

"IT HURTS WHEN YOU HAVE TO SMILE AND YOU DON'T WANT TO SMILE,
BUT THE BEST THING TO DO IS TO SMILE."
—MARY J. BLIGE, SINGER AND SONGWRITER

Lesson Learned – Don't wait to get shit done. If something is weighing on you, address it. The longer you put something off, the more it weighs on you. The more it will suck your soul and dig deeper into you.

Highest High – A reason to smile is that I finally fixed my front tooth that had been bothering me for years now. It wasn't a huge deal, but at the same time, it was. I wouldn't smile fully. I lacked confidence in social settings as a result, and it weighed on me. That lack of smiling was similar to how alcohol had begun to control me at an unconscious level.

Owen,

The unconscious mind is so powerful, yet so hard to understand, so hard to control or at least work with. It's 10 times more powerful than the conscious mind, but most of us aren't even aware it exists.

One of the best ways I've heard the unconscious mind explained is that if someone asked you to think of your cell phone number you could instantly think of it. But you weren't at that moment until I asked you to think of it. That's because it was stored in your unconscious mind. That makes sense.

Well, you're four, so probably not. If I told you to think about Spider-Man you could, but you weren't thinking about him until I asked you to do so. There, that's better.

The problem with this thinking is that there are so many ideas and thoughts in our unconscious mind that we are unaware they even exist, like with my drinking.

This Naked Mind talks about this every time it references what it calls liminal points within the book. Their breakdown says that only our belief system occurs within the conscious mind. The other three parts of our thinking, experiences and observations, assumptions, even conclusions all usually exist unconsciously.

We all have the beliefs I referenced in other days unconsciously like "drinking makes me more fun," or "I only have a good time when I drink," or "drinking makes me a better dancer." These beliefs differ for everyone, but in reality, it's all bullshit.

It's not true; it's just that our unconscious mind has perceived it to be true through false reinforcements. Therefore, now our conscious mind perceives it to be true.

Where the fuck am I going with all of this? Well, little did I know how much the front tooth I referenced at the top of the day was affecting me unconsciously.

It was discolored and misshapen. I didn't think it looked good; I know it didn't feel good. I know consciously I wouldn't smile fully in pictures. I lacked confidence in social settings. Hell, I lacked confidence in general as a result of it.

But insurance would only cover a new tooth every 5 years. I let the last dentist off the hook by just accepting it even though I knew at the time it didn't look good, and it didn't feel good.

Fast forward to Monday of this week. I had had enough. Ironically, my sobriety gave me the confidence, or the drive, to say I'm tired of looking at this tooth. I don't care if I have to pay a few hundred dollars extra to get this tooth fixed. I'm done having it in my mouth.

Today, I went in and got it fixed.

Alcohol played a part in that, or it used to. It can control you in such bizarre ways including financially. When you drink heavily, you don't mind dropping $80 or $100 on a tab in a night. You don't even bat an eye really. You would spend $1,000 over the course of a month on alcohol, and that's light for a heavy drinker.

But you wouldn't think about putting that aside and fixing your tooth, or a problem with your car, or whatever the small thing is in your life that's now turned into a big thing. Alcohol grabs you like that. You want to spend time with your friend. You want to spend money on your friend. It's stupid. It's unhealthy. It's controlling. It's debilitating.

Anyway, I'm so happy to have my tooth fixed, my swagger back, and my full smile once again. A full smile for the first time in three years!

The last time I was really willing to smile was in 2017.

I was starting to dig through a lot of reasons why I've been unhappy lately, unsatisfied, but a big one was my actual smile. My front right tooth is fake from an old basketball injury, an elbow to the front tooth that killed it and required a replacement.

In August 29, 2017, I went to a bad dentist and have been afraid to smile ever since. The tooth they put in was colored incorrectly, didn't fit right, and I wasn't confident enough to speak up and say something.

As a result, when I did smile it was always a half smile or a smirk. I would never fully smile, which always weighed on me because I have a great smile even a cute little dimple I gave myself when I was five.

The point of this quick aside is to tell you that not only have I been working a ton lately on fixing myself, looking within, on giving myself more reasons to smile but I also decided to go to the dentist to get a front tooth fixed that had been bothering me for years, and it looks great! I'm not afraid to smile anymore.

What's holding you back from finding that joy in your life? What's the smile that's gone missing in your life? What are the little things in your life that don't seem like a big deal but keep adding up and stealing your joy? Start to dig deep, look within, and don't be afraid to smile. I believe in life we are all exactly where we are supposed to be; we are all perfect.

But you also can't be afraid to take those leaps, to make those changes, and to give yourself that love and that confidence moving forward that you deserve!

DAY 20

A First Date

Lesson Learned – Danielle and I are starting over. The love and depth of our relationship is still there. That's good and bad—the deep feeling of love and then resentment. More than anything, we are going to have to learn to love all over again, in a different and healthier way, if it's to work.

Highest High – Diving deeper into the lesson of the day learned, Danielle and I decide to try an actual "first date" tonight. We head to an authentic Mexican spot with an entire vegan menu. She's high though. That sends the date down a path I hadn't anticipated.

Owen,

It's Friday today, a day of firsts. First full day with my new tooth. First Friday I've taught back-to-back yoga classes and felt clean. Totally back on top of my game and in a good space. Danielle and I also decide to try out a first date.

She reaches out around 5 p.m. and asks what I'm doing tonight. She then mentions a little Mexican spot that's about 20 minutes away. We had talked about a date night on Saturday night so that we could sleep in Sunday morning, but it got bumped up to tonight.

Danielle arrives around 7:30 p.m. and is high for the first time since I've been sober, which is a little weird at first. I can always tell when she's high. She could always tell when I was drunk or had been drinking.

She said she's been trying to cut back on alcohol and weed, both, since I stopped drinking but her roommate wanted to smoke, so she did too. I don't think much of it at first as it doesn't bother me, but it leads to some deeper thoughts later in the night.

We head to this Mexican food spot, and it's real Mexican food. They sell tongues and assorted authentic foods like that. The tacos only have onions, cilantro, and meat on them with limes and rice and beans on the side. None of that fluffy American stuff we put on them. Those two pieces let you know you're at an authentic Mexican restaurant.

Danielle had eaten a bunch of chips and salsa. She was high resulting in quite a bit of her main dish being leftover. I smashed all of my delicious tacos and then we headed home.

It was only 9 p.m. or so once we arrived back at the house. We get in bed and just lay there talking and snuggling. We're both pretty full, and we've been going at it sexually pretty consistently for the last week or so. We mess around a little bit but not much. We decide to just call it a night.

It's strange having a first date like this, totally sober. I know it's strange to say, but we're having to relearn a lot of things about each other. Or perhaps unlearn might be a better word here.

One of my favorite quotes talks about how "learning is an external act; unlearning is an internal one." This feels a bit like we are unlearning some things about ourselves and our relationship. That's healthy. That's also hard to do.

Habits have been established; behaviors have been formed. These topics vary from trust to love, to communication, to her smoking and my drinking. My drinking is gone, but she has smoked tonight.

I do genuinely believe her in that she wouldn't have smoked weed if it wasn't for her roommate asking her to smoke. Danielle has been good around me to this point. Hell, it was her idea for me to get sober. She'd prefer me that way. I do too.

That shows the power of who we surround ourselves with and how those people affect our decision-making. Danielle certainly didn't cause me to drink too much as I was on my way before we met. It worsened and eventually had to stop.

It's also true that one of the reasons it started to escalate in the end was that there were many days when she would smoke weed at 8 or 9 a.m. I then thought, in my distorted thinking, that it was socially acceptable for me to start drinking beers at 11 a.m. or noon.

Danielle's thing is weed, and mine is alcohol. She's smoking and therefore I can start drinking. It's all good.

No, it's not. That's not normal, either of our behaviors.

This is the impact that your partner, your roommate, or your friend can have on you and your habits and decisions.

I think back to college when I had two roommates. All three of us drank heavily. There was a really good chance that one of us wanted to drink on any given night. That meant all that person had to do was convince one of the others to drink and if they succeeded in that then the last one would drink too. We'd cave to the peer pressure.

You'll feel this as you get older. Pressure to make poor decisions from your high school and college teammates. Pressure to do things from a shitty partner or a cousin or whoever else it may be. Our lives are filled with a number of these difficult decisions. What do we give into socially, and how does that start to affect our decision-making as our life progresses?

The most difficult part of it all is that every time you say yes, it gets easier to say yes again. Every time you drink or smoke or skip a class or whatever negative decision you feel pressured into experimenting with, it is easier to repeat that destructive behavior.

That's why we must be so conscious about who we surround ourselves with, the people we let in our inner circle, and the habits they have already established. As they so often say, we are often the equivalent of the five people we spend the most time with, so take inventory. Who are those five people for you? What are their habits? What does their future look like?

It also reminds me of a girl I dated at Eastern Arizona College. Serena was her name and after Cassie from SBU, she was the next serious girlfriend I had in life.

Serena was an actual model from a tiny town in Arizona called Safford. While I can't recall our first date, like above, I can recall what most of them consisted of. It was heavy drinking, sex, and some surface-level conversations at whatever party we could find that night.

Our relationship was the definition of a superficial one—one of those centered around bad habits and bad people, but it was an important one for me to experience. I was the assistant coach at the time at EAC as they called it. We were the Gila Monsters—the only one in the country!

I was 23. She was 18.

She stood 5'10, had long dark hair, and was Hispanic though she didn't know how much exactly. She wasn't proud of that piece of her heritage, so she never tried to find out.

Living in Arizona and being part Mexican, she always had a nice golden skin tone, big boobs, and long hair. If I'd have drawn up a physical image of who I thought I wanted to spend the rest of my life with, she would have been damn close to that image. She was beautiful physically in every way.

As an assistant at Eastern Arizona College, I'd work 50–60 hour weeks. I taught a few classes at the junior college. We'd have workouts and practice every day, watch in-season films, had recruiting, and then class checks for our players. You wear a lot of hats when you are an assistant coach at the junior college level.

I'd usually get done for the night around 9 p.m.

Then Serena and I would start drinking; we'd start partying. That would go on until 12 or 1 a.m. in the morning on a light night and 3 or 4 a.m. on a heavy night. And we could both really drink. Splitting a fifth or an 18-pack of beer was a pretty common amount of alcohol for us even on our laid-back nights.

This pattern continued for around six months until one night I was sitting at a bonfire with her. It was a random Tuesday night at like 2 a.m.

I had taught an 8 a.m. class to start that day. I was tired as hell, pretty buzzed, and just wanted to go home, have sex, and call it a night.

But she wasn't ready to call it a night.

Just like that, I remember thinking to myself, what the fuck are you doing with this girl? Our conversations were superficial as could be, which shouldn't be shocking dating an 18-year-old. I know.

We were constantly talking about drinking or what we'd do in the future with money, and I say that judgement-free. We were constantly around people that didn't challenge us, make us better, or provide us growth in any kind of way.

These friends didn't mean bad, but that's the challenge. Negative people don't mean to hurt you. In fact, they usually are trying to get better to the best of their awareness. We all think that we are improving in some way, or else we'd change. But the reality is that some people drag you down and don't lift you up. This relationship and those around us were weighing me down.

I realize now it wasn't her fault at all. She was just getting started in the modeling industry at this time. She would gain some traction a few years later, and that was the kind of life she wanted to live. That was the kind of life she was used to living.

But I knew, even at that time, that I needed to make changes in my life to be successful, to be the person, the coach, and the partner that I wanted to be. So we broke up.

That was the last time I dated someone exclusively for looks, and that's also the other lesson for you today. Check your inner circle, the habits, the thoughts, and the development of the people around you. Don't date exclusively for looks or for the sex even.

Looks are important, attraction is important, and sex is great. To me, it gets you through some difficult times when you have a strong physical attraction. I also think staying physically fit for your partner is a sort of unconscious nod toward them showing them you appreciate them by keeping your body and appearance at a level that you know will be enjoyable for them.

But the mind has to be there too. It won't take you many dates to figure that out. It won't take you too many dates to figure out if you find that connection, physically and mentally. If they care for you, if they're kind, or if they like to grow themselves, mentally and physically. Do you share common interests?

One final piece on dating and inner circles before we finish up today. This last piece combines the two.

Does your partner have a good relationship with their family and those closest to them? These are the people that know them and know their character best. If you realize your partner is acting differently when around these people then you don't really know your partner.

I learned that one the hard way. A girl I dated later in life was always way different around her family than she was with me. Turns out I had it backward. Who she was around her family was the real her, and who she was around me was the fake version of her.

You start to figure out all these things as you go. Like life, like so many things we've talked about in this book, it takes repetition and experience to learn how to date, how to love, and how to be loved.

Usually it takes several dates, months, or years to figure out if you have a long-term chemistry with someone.

Sometimes, it takes one date and you think to yourself, "Fuck no." That's fine too; move on.

Whatever you do, relax and enjoy your dating life, and stay present as you experience it. Know that it's not only the physical component that makes a date, a relationship, or a partnership work. Be intentional about what you're looking for, what makes you happy.

Then pay attention to the details of your roommates, your friends, and those around you. By doing so, you are looking at the person you will become in life.

These friends, these partners, and these family members will be the ones that lift and grow you to new heights. Or they'll be the ones that smoke enough, drink enough, and are just lazy enough to keep you right where you are at. You decide.

DAY 21

Darkness Wins; I Lose

"NEVER CONFUSE A SINGLE DEFEAT WITH A FINAL DEFEAT."
—F. SCOTT FITZGERALD, NOVELIST

Lesson Learned – Yoga was the base of how my relationship with Danielle started. It's interesting to revisit it at a deeper level now that she and I are both in a different space relationship-wise and as individuals.

Lowest Low – One of the most awkward feelings in the world is lying in bed with someone that you've had sex with, are in love with, but are also unsure if it's going to work. That awkward space and the awkward energy is tangible and painful.

Owen,

Tough calls, emotional responses, and tons of feelings involved. That's how today started. That's how this day would end. I remember another day that was like that. It was one of the worst and most confusing days of my life. I still don't understand what happened. I never will.

More on that later on in the day.

Today, I woke up with Danielle after our first date, and we lay around in bed kissing and touching. We're playing around in bed like you will with a partner one of these days. Those innocent and playful experiences can feel incredible when things are going well. If they're not, they can feel awkward.

Today is an awkward day for Danielle. She's emotional, upset, and confused with her emotions. That's confusing for me too. I'm unsure of what to do other than giving her space. I get a text at around 10 a.m. asking when I'm going to hop on a zoom call that I had written down for 1 p.m. Turns out the old time was 1 p.m., and it had been rescheduled to today, a Saturday, at 10 a.m.

Shit.

I make it work though and the call ends. I go to meet up with Danielle. She's gone to practice with some yoga teachers that are going through their training. The session ends, and we go our separate ways, almost awkwardly.

I can tell Danielle is trying to guard herself against showing affection to me in public especially around others that know us both and our past, which most of these teachers in training do. That's fine. I respect that and her space. It does make it a little challenging for me on how to act. It does make me feel guilty.

She ends up calling me about 15 minutes later on her way home. She asked how I felt, and I said I was cool with everything. I tell her there was a moment when we both left in the parking lot where I thought she'd at least come talk to me and tell me how the class and practice was for her and what she was doing for lunch. But she clearly wanted space.

I say all of that to her on the phone, and she agrees. It's a strange space to be in right now wondering what she is thinking and not being able to discuss it in public. It's our new normal, but I don't like it.

Eventually, I ask Danielle to come back over later that night. She says she's thinking about it critically. This is around 8 p.m.

She doesn't. She decides instead to go to bed. We don't talk again until early the next morning.

The physical practice was good today, but I can always tell when I'm off balance with my personal work. I didn't read enough, and I didn't write enough today.

One of the challenges in wanting to spend time and be with Danielle is that it throws off my balance somewhat, and I haven't figured out how to navigate that yet. I have to do a better job of feeling and showing her love but not letting it become an unhealthy obsession or get lopsided time-wise. That's easier said than done.

I know now that I need to go to a meeting tomorrow and work on myself, have some conversations with some others that are like-minded and have been where I am at, felt what I have felt. That part is nice about meetings. You get to have conversations with people that have been there. It's grounding and centering for me.

Danielle holds that space for me, like you do, Owen, but when she's trying to establish what is healthy for her, that makes it challenging for us both.

She and I want to spend a ton of time with each other, and when we do, it feels amazing. We also know that's not healthy. We have to balance our time, balance our emotions, and balance our love for each other.

I can almost feel her physically and emotionally pulling away today, and that's really hard. I notice it. I sense it.

We'll see what tomorrow brings and how she and I continue to navigate all of this. I know I need a meeting. I'm supposed to practice yoga again with that training group tomorrow. I also teach in the morning.

I'll have more answers tomorrow. I need to learn to find answers about me every day. Not just focusing on the relationship although that's hard.

Read, write, journal, a physical practice. Read, write, journal, a physical practice. Every day. I see it. I just have to apply it.

I'm reminded of how in my most difficult times, I throw myself into work—some kind of work. This time it's healing myself. The last time something this heavy happened, I threw myself into my coaching.

The year was 2006, and I was in my second season now at Eastern Arizona College. I was sitting in an airport, eating a double cheeseburger from Burger King, headed back from our Christmas Break as a team.

The other assistant, Anthony, was already back. He was 22, and I was 24—the wise veteran coach between the two of us. This was Anthony's first coaching job, but even for him, he was being weird—mumbling almost incoherently about the fact that our head coach had found his wife and their two-year-old son dead in their garage.

I said, "What do you mean they're dead? Are you sure?"

"Yeah, pretty sure." He's obviously still unsure.

"Did coach kill them?" I ask. Thinking surely not, but how does something like this happen? There would be no easy answers, no satisfactory answers, no matter what actually happened.

A few hours later, I was back asking questions to everyone involved, trying to find out what I could and trying to make sense of it all.

The reality of the situation was the head coach, Tim, and his wife had been going through a nasty divorce for a number of disturbing reasons and were separated. Tim went back to get his son for the day. What he thought would just be another normal day.

He found them both dead. His wife had killed herself and their two-year-old by locking themselves in the garage and letting the car run until the carbon dioxide filled their lungs causing them to pass out and then die.

She had their two-year-old sign the suicide note he found in the car along with a glass of milk in a sippy cup. The milk was to make their two-year-old feel better about being in his car seat. That's some cold-hearted shit.

Weeks later, the head coach would try and get me to read the suicide note she left him. (She also mailed six copies of it around the country to other family members to spite him), but I wouldn't read it. I still haven't.

I'll never forget walking into the head coach's house the first time I got back into town. The house where it all happened. It was so eerie. It felt like a ghost was around, some type of energy that you could almost walk through.

The head coach, Tim; our athletic director, Anthony; and the head coach's best friend, Kelly, were there. Kelly also happened to be the head coach of our biggest rival within the conference. Rivalries fall away when shit like this happens.

I don't think I even hugged Tim. I remember walking in, but I was so unsure of what to do. I think I just sat on the other side of the room, observing. I'd learn a little about what happened, but details would be foggy. Everyone was afraid to ask and talk about what was going on.

One of the things I did learn was that I was now the interim head coach of the team at the age of 24. We had players on the team that were 21.

I was still a baby but now in charge. I needed to remain strong, show leadership, and show toughness. I don't think I even cried—not that first day, not the day I first spoke to the team as the interim head coach, and not even at the funeral of the two-year-old boy. Anthony was emotional, and I felt like one of us needed to keep it together for the guys to see what toughness and leadership looks like in difficult times.

I realize now how unhealthy it was to bottle up all those emotions— to be afraid to feel and to be afraid to cry. That's what we're taught as athletes and coaches: don't feel; don't show emotion; be a robot.

That's bullshit.

We should feel. We're human.

We should show emotion. We're human.

We should understand it's normal to express those emotions from time to time. Whether that's in our personal lives, on the court, or for fuck's sake at a funeral of a two-year-old boy who's just been murdered. We all need to understand it's OK to feel, show, and then discuss our emotions.

But I didn't do it then. I didn't think I should. And you know what? I bet most people in and around the program would say that I handled things right. That's how I should have handled it. That's what's broken about athletics.

I went on to be the head coach for two weeks. I was the head coach for one game against a JV team from the Phoenix area. We'd won the game by 20. I'll forever be 1–0 as a head coach—undefeated.

The head coach would come back to coach the rest of the season, amazingly, surprisingly. He often talked about how that was the only way for him to move on with his life. It was the only way for him to stay busy.

The team even more incredibly went on to win the conference that season and play in the region championship game before losing to that team I spoke about earlier with the rival head coach, Arizona Western.

Over the course of that year and into the spring, the head coach stayed in that same house his son was murdered. Anthony and I would go visit him, have a few beers by the fire pit, and play video games. His son's room remained untouched. I wouldn't look in there. I wouldn't go in the garage either. I can only imagine the weight, the heaviness he must have felt through it all. It had to be unbearable.

Tim and I got along really well. Our past, even our coaching career to this point, was similar. We both played NCAA Division II basketball in the same conference and had grown up in the Midwest.

And both of our minds worked analytically. He was ahead of his time in that regard. One of the first books he recommended to me was *Moneyball*, that analytical behind-the-scenes look on the professional baseball team—the Oakland Athletics. He coached analytically too. It was about the team not an individual. We had a great relationship before all of this happened.

But I started to notice a shift in our relationship over the next few weeks and months. I was probably his closest friend there in the city, the one he spoke with most frequently, at least. His son was gone—murdered by his wife. We had lost the regional championship game at home. He had nothing to keep his mind busy anymore, nothing and no one to take these dark thoughts out on or to speak to them about.

I think he took them out on me, probably unconsciously in the end.

Months later, the relationship between the head coach and I became so strained that I looked for other coaching jobs in the spring and found one at Seward County. I applied thinking I wouldn't get it. I ended up getting the job. I moved in June.

Tim was one of the best coaches I ever worked for. He and the head coach at Seward were the two best although they couldn't have been more different.

Tim and I would end our relationship there on rocky terms not speaking much the next season. He'd be fired the next year too. He was accused and found guilty of sleeping with a minor. It was messy.

If I would have stayed, I would have become the head coach of EAC that next season on what was a really talented team. Another ripple effect.

Focus on the emotional part on this day, Owen, and don't be afraid to feel, to be in touch with your emotions. It's OK to laugh, but it's also OK to cry. It's good, actually.

We can feel things as athletes. We can succeed, and we can fail. But we're human; we're not robots. Acting like we are robots only causes more pain and develops bad and unhealthy habits—habits like drinking alcohol to numb your pain.

Week 4

Love

DAY 22

Witnessing Relapse

Lesson Learned – Keep doing the work. When you feel good or when you feel bad continue to build that self-love and self-care.

Lowest Low (for Barry) – Today at a meeting, a man showed up drunk. He had called one of the long-time sober attendees from the group to come get him and to help him get sober. It was bizarre to witness.

Owen,

Today started off with my first official "Best of Sunday Flow." I decided this past week to put together a "best of" music, movements, and teaching from the entire month into one powerful class. It was remarkable! The class loved it. I had fun, and they were worn out. It was great.

Then something strange happened. Danielle was thinking about coming by last night but didn't as we've been taking it slow.

She and I were trying to help another student learn to teach yoga today, but the student was really struggling. She was intimidated that people outside their training group showed up to her teach-back, so Danielle and I hid off to the side as she taught.

Something wasn't quite right though as we sat off to the side, so I eventually just got up and left as I wasn't going to practice with this instructor anyway.

I went home, showered, and ate. I did some much-needed reading and writing as my mind was racing a little bit. Reading and writing always helps to calm the mind just like meditation does.

A couple hours later Danielle reached out as I had left my necklace up at the studio. She asked if she could bring it by and grab a computer charger that she had left at my place weeks ago. I, of course, said. "Sure, stop by. I'd love to see you."

And sure enough, when she arrived, she was half-joking and half-serious that this weekend she had intended to let me know she needed space. We needed to back off of talking again. Emotions had become too strong for her, and she continued to struggle to see a path forward for us in the long term.

I gave her space to finish, was careful again not to react, and simply let her speak her mind. In this case, it was apparent to me she was just processing some strong emotions. She had just stayed the night on Friday, and we spent most of yesterday together, awkwardly. All that scared her.

It's become evident this will take space and lots of time and even then it might not work. She was able to see that too. We talked through everything—how I love her, how I am a very different person, and that it is going to be hard as hell, really hard to make this work. But it will also be worth it, at least in my eyes. It feels like that's to be determined in hers.

While it is all about one day at a time, neither of us would currently be pursuing this (all of this) right now if we didn't see the potential in how incredible it could be.

This part of the relationship reminds me of coaching a super talented athlete that's raw as hell but not picking up on the coaching and not picking up on the system you've put in place.

As a coach and as a partner, you want to be patient and see the process through. There also comes a point where it's too much, and where it's not working for either side anymore.

After an hour or so of talking, we both left in a good space, a loving space. We agreed that we will move forward slowly just as we have been doing. This feels different, much different, in a healthy way.

We agree to build on that love, that trust, and that gratitude as we start to rebuild the foundation of our home that's been swept away at this point—a storm of lust, alcohol, and unhealthy habits and communication.

Later, I head to a meeting at 4 p.m., and it's the biggest meeting I've been to up to this point. Over 20 people are there at an outside meeting, socially distanced. COVID is happening right now and sweeping through Overland Park. That limits attendance with everything in life, even recovery meetings.

There's a guy there, Barry, that seems drunk. I can't tell if he's fucked up from past drugs and alcohol or currently drunk.

Turns out Barry is drunk.

He had called one of the senior most sober members of the group (18 years sober) and asked him if he would come and get him because he couldn't drive and was too drunk, but he wanted the misery to end. There were no suicidal thoughts or anything. He was just tired of being a drunk.

I can empathize with that.

Barry wanted to start his recovery right at that moment. Kudos to him for giving it a try... Again.

We all go around and speak into the topic today, which, not ironically, was the question: What brought everyone at the meeting today to surrender to their problems? It was a great conversation.

Barry admitted to being drunk and that he was currently bottoming out. As I recently learned, that process is an extremely difficult one, and it's usually day three or four later before you truly bottom out. The alcohol has to leave your system, and you have to lose your friend—your precious alcohol—before the healing can begin. That takes time and sobriety. I wish him the best.

There was some good conversation today like I mentioned. For a lot of people, striving to be perfect led them to recovery—being too smart and too strong to be an addict, and their ego coming in the way. These were the same things I struggled with in my recovery and alcohol consumption. It's gotten easier up to this point as the days pass. It is still hard but considerably easier as time passes.

Once you surrender to all the most difficult pieces, day-to-day existence isn't as complicated. Things calm down and clarity ensues.

The beauty of the day, the sun on your face, the skin, the smell, conversations you took for granted, and the kiss of a loved one all become a different kind of intoxication. You discover a gratitude for all the amazing things we all have in our lives. Your sobriety becomes incredible. It's just hard as fuck to get there when you're in the darkness just like my man, Barry, showed us during the meeting.

Barry said he's been on and off the sobriety wagon many times. He was super critical of himself. As a result, he was saying all the things I said in the beginning like he didn't deserve love, that he was fucking up, and that he didn't think he could do it.

I never thought I couldn't stop. I just didn't know why I should. I didn't love myself enough to stop.

Time will tell if he's serious this time, if he's really bottomed out. Percentages show it takes multiple times for most people to recover and even then, more often than not, they will still relapse.

That knowledge keeps me reading and writing daily, going to meetings, and showing gratitude for my journey and where I'm at today. I don't want to be back there where my guy Barry was at today.

Barry's story is similar and yet different to the ones I saw as a junior college coach. Not the addiction part but the failure to see the destructive habits that were killing so many of the athletes I was coaching.

The season I spoke about yesterday at Eastern Arizona in 2006 had one of the most talented players I ever coached on the team. A 6'8 physical freak—a chiseled body, great athleticism, tough as hell, and he could even shoot out to the three-point line, which at that time was still uncommon for big men. Travis was his name.

Travis had bounced around. He needed multiple schools over the past few years and was looking for some stability in his life and in his athletic career. He wouldn't find it.

Every day was a challenge with him. It was such a challenge that the head coach put Travis in the dorm that I was in charge of just so I could keep an eye on him.

My dorm was an overflow dorm. It was used only for the first few weeks of school until enough students dropped out that the school could fit all the students into the three dorms that were regularly used.

Travis was going to stay in my dorm for as long as the school would let him.

On the court, he played hard. He was pretty coachable, took direction, and played physical. But he was still raw. He didn't have great body control yet so he got in foul trouble on the defensive end. It also caused him to have turnovers on the offensive end.

Off the court, he was off the chain as kids said back then. He smoked weed, drank heavily, would try and sneak his girlfriend into the dorms, would fight other athletes and students, was accused of stealing at one point—anything was on the table for him.

I remember vividly going to check on him in his room one night although it was not a surprise inspection or anything like that. I was smarter than to do that knowing I would have found something. This was just me walking into his room to talk with him when his door was open.

There was broken up weed on his dorm room desk.

I said, "Travis, what the fuck are you doing?"

"What?" he said naively. I genuinely feel he didn't think he was doing anything wrong.

This happens a lot at the juco level when athletes come from places where illegal behaviors and negative behaviors are not only tolerated but commonplace. Like with some of my behaviors these incredible athletes learn to think what they are doing isn't bad, or wrong, but normal.

"That's weed!" I shouted.

"No, it isn't," he responded, saying it in a way like you would say to me about not putting your toys away or taking a piece of candy you know you shouldn't be eating. However, you're four. He was 20, and this was an illegal drug in plain sight not a Starburst.

"Travis, I know that's weed. My roommate in college sold weed and smoked every day. I know what broken up weed looks like."

"Oh, it's not mine," he said, finally giving into the fact that it was weed, and he was busted.

As a side note, my roommate in college did sell and smoke weed quite frequently. I was so much in fact that he served two weeks in jail over winter break at Southwest Baptist University over a combination of a weed distribution charge and then a DUI that violated his probation.

Being the Godly school that SBU was, he served his two weeks and then rejoined the team in January. God is good and a basketball fan, apparently.

Back to Travis. I didn't even tell the head coach. What you hear a lot when you are a juco assistant is something along the lines of, "Take care of it, and I don't want to hear about it."

After the tenth time of hearing something like this from the head coach at Eastern Arizona about Travis, I started making executive decisions on my own. I was not telling the head coach anything and sweeping lots of behaviors and actions of his under the rug.

Athletes quickly learn that these behaviors are probably wrong but don't usually hold repercussions for them as they would for others. That's accurate.

In the case of Travis, he couldn't get out of his own way, and his behaviors were too extreme. A couple weeks before our first game, there was a gigantic fight between our football team, who was a top 25 level team, and another top 25 team at home. It was going to be a super intense game and everyone on campus knew that especially the athletes.

What was a back-and-forth game ended with a gigantic brawl on the field. I don't even remember who won; it doesn't matter.

Travis, as you might imagine, was in the middle of the fight. He threw punches, and he might have even hit someone with a helmet. I can't remember the exact details but it was caught on camera, and bad enough, our head coach didn't even try and appeal. Travis was sent home the next week.

Every year there are thousands, literally thousands, of athletes that are high major talent types of athletes. Their stories are never told and never heard. Thousands of Travis-type athletes that can't get their shit together get kicked out of their school and get sent back home.

To me, this is why we need to push for more mental training and more mindfulness training for athletes. Imagine how powerful it would be if every time an athlete stepped on campus for the first time they couldn't do anything, practice or play, until we checked on them mentally.

We do physicals, but why don't we do mental check-ins?

All we are doing by ignoring the mental side of things is setting athletes up to fail, to repeat toxic behaviors, and to relapse just like Barry.

My goal is to help athletes and coaches on this journey to have the understanding of their minds, of staying calm and collected, and staying present. I want to help athletes not rely on drugs or alcohol to calm the mind or not feel. I did that, but it doesn't work.

I'll do the same with you, Owen. I don't know that it will work; no one does.

I do know that I'll do everything I can to try and put you in the best possible space I can as a father—physically, yes, but, more importantly, mentally too.

DAY 23

Tough Love and Success

"GO AFTER SOMETHING YOU REALLY LOVE AND FIND A WAY TO MAKE
THAT WORK FOR YOU, AND THEN YOU'LL BE A HAPPY PERSON."
—TOM PETTY, MUSICIAN

Lesson Learned – I'm going to pick a sponsor today and see if that helps in recovery for me. My sister, Nikki, anticipated who it would be from the beginning—a guy that rubbed me the wrong way that first day, at that initial meeting. Perhaps that's what I need right now—discipline, work ethic, and a belief in the practice combined with a kind of tough love.

Highest High – Your mom and I are in a much better space, and it's nice to see that relationship healing as that will be really important for all of us as a family moving forward. It brings me joy to see us co-parenting successfully again.

Owen,

It was a good day today for me and for my recovery. I had a big call today in the afternoon with a high-level Division I program that went well. I talked to the entire team minus a couple players.

If this bid goes through from the price range of $3,500 to $10,000 that will be the biggest month I've had to date business-wise. That's counting the fact that I already completed a $3,500 sale and have the potential to get up to $20,000 in awards from a start-up/accelerator here locally.

That would mean a $30,000 plus month for me and for MindSport. That's starting to get some real traction.

I then headed to teach a yoga class this morning, which wasn't quite full but went well. Things move and flow so much more fluidly now. I have a grasp for names, movements, cues, and music. Everything is so much clearer for me now.

I finalized a workshop today too—an inversion workshop. It's less than two weeks away, and I have no idea how the turnout will look. It's also on your birthday, but I think I navigated around that in a really successful way so that everyone wins, and I can still hold the workshop.

Originally, when I was planning for the workshop, I saw that I wasn't supposed to have you for the weekend. So I planned the workshop for your birthday, the 12th. That way, I don't have to sit around and mope while I don't have you on your birthday. Then I remembered to check the parenting plan because your mom and I alternate who gets you on your birthday. This year happens to be the year that I get you for your birthday—even numbered years.

When I picked you up from school, I saw that your mom had already sent out invitations for everyone to come to a party on your birthday at a waterpark. It turns out she had already invited 30+ families to this party.

I immediately text your mom and let her know that I was supposed to have you this year, but I wanted her to still be able to host the party. Let's just figure out a way to switch dates, I said.

A conflict like this would have been a problem in the past, early on in our divorce. Negotiating days, switching times, etc. It would have all been a big hassle.

Instead, I let your mom know that I appreciate that she had planned the party and that my sister, Megan, was coming to Springfield with her family days before his birthday. Let's just figure out a way to switch another day. I'll take Owen for those three days, and it will be all good.

Only an hour or so passed, and everyone agreed. That was easy! It was nice to be able to have a conversation about co-parenting in a healthy way. Another area of my life that's a work in progress.

I end the day by picking a sponsor that's a tough love kind of guy. Ken is his name. He's been sober for almost 16 years with no breaks in his sobriety. I'm still unsure about the forever piece of this, even that line of thinking, but I do know alcohol can no longer be a part of my life. Because of that I choose someone that's done what I'm trying to accomplish. Ken is that guy.

I struggle with no-nonsense type of people like Ken where it's their way or the highway. He's a thoughtful guy but is also very rigid in his behaviors and his outlook on the program. Similar to my sister Nikki and her husband Jim. That's the challenging part; it's also most likely what I need.

I need a shift in my thinking, in how I've been doing things. So I'm willing to give it a try.

Ken reminds me of the coach I worked for immediately after Eastern Arizona College when I took the assistant job that next season at Seward County Community College. Bryan Zollinger was his name, Coach Z, and he just took the job over in the summer of 2007. I was the assistant he hired once he took the job.

Seward is a prestigious junior college basketball program with several national tournament appearances. It is one of the best juco basketball facilities in the country and a supportive community. It's a great job for the head coach and his assistant, both.

Coach Z had played at Seward on a team that finished 3rd in the country. He was hired back to restore the program after they had fallen on hard times as the coach before him had become lazy in his accountability of his players. The team we took over was supremely talented but had no discipline whatsoever. The return players were in for a rude awakening.

We still had several spots to fill once we took over the roster and did a good job filling those spots. We signed a freshman point guard names Reggie Chamberlain who would go on to be freshman of the year in the incredibly talented Jayhawk Conference. Chamberlain went on to play at Wichita State and then finish his career at UMKC.

Next, we signed a Brazilian sharpshooter, Bruno Mendes. We filled in some bench spots with some good in-state talent, which is important in that conference.

They had some complimentary big men from the previous regime including a player named Darko Cohadarevic. Darko was a 6'9 Serbian that could shoot threes and do work in the post. He was a phenomenal junior college talent, and he would end up being an All-American.

But he was like a wild stallion that needed to be broken. Several of the players from the previous coach needed to be broken. Sometimes coaches have to break down their athletes' minds, or so they think, before they can build them back up.

I'm not sure this is true, and there has to be balance there in which you can both nurture the conscious mind while breaking down the unconscious mind. But in athletics, it has to happen much faster especially at the juco level. You'd need someone half crazy but smart as hell. Someone that was strong, tough, intelligent, and not afraid to stick to his guns.

Coach Z was the man for the job.

We had the team do everything from team-building exercises with zip lines, trust falls, and climbing poles to having them flip tires and push trucks in neutral around a circle drive. We ran 132 sprints one day in practice. I counted. This was all just in the preseason.

The 132 sprints might be my favorite story from that season—a season that was wildly successful and ended up with a 3rd place finish at the national tournament. A 32-6 season and one of the best seasons if not the best season in school history.

On this particular day, this particular practice, Darko was trying to show that he was just as tough and just as stubborn as Coach Z. That was a poor idea.

We were running a basic drill, and I had asked Darko to touch a line. He said he did; I said he didn't, and we went back and forth for a while until Coach Z stopped the practice.

This was a pivotal moment for a couple reasons. At the collegiate athletic level, there can be some discussion on some points, but ultimately there has to remain an order of accountability. A pecking order that went as follows: the head coach, the assistant, and then the players. When direction is given you can't have players talking back or barking at the assistant coach and definitely not at the head coach.

This relationship has to be one of respect though. That's where most assistant and head coaches get it wrong. Bad coaches see this relationship as a power trip. They want to dominate or belittle players just to show strength, to try and show dominance over someone that they can only hold power over because of a title. That's the wrong way to do it.

Players must respect you and for the right reasons. Z and I were trying to do that with this team—show them discipline, show them toughness, but in a respectful way. But getting anyone out of their comfort zone is difficult. Being held accountable can suck. I was holding Darko accountable then finally Coach Z had to stop practice and do the same by letting him know once I told him to do something that it wasn't a discussion. It simply needed to be done.

Coach Z did not communicate the message in that tone or that language. I'm sure it was much rougher around the edges, probably involving cussing, but that was the point we were both trying to get across to Darko.

Darko decided on this day he was going to draw a line in the sand. He wasn't going to do things our way. As I mentioned, he wanted to prove he was just as tough and stubborn as Z, and so he kept talking back to us both. Coach Z had the entire team get on the line and run six sprints in six sprints in 35 seconds. That's tough to do. Most people, even good athletes, couldn't do that once.

We'd do that several more times on this day.

After the first set of six, Coach Z asked Darko, "You done now?"

Darko said, "Nope."

Coach Z said, "OK, back on the line."

They ran again.

"Anything else?" Z asked.

"Whatever man," Darko responded.

"Back on the line," Z said. Coach Z was now sitting in the stands. Coaches usually coach practice on the court. Z was now getting comfortable. He knew he wasn't going anywhere for a while—grab a Snickers as the commercial says.

Anytime anyone said anything, anytime anyone missed touching a line during a sprint, anytime anyone on the team did anything—no matter how small the detail—on this day, we ran again.

Soon Z would have them start running 10 sprints instead of 6, 60 seconds now instead of 35. The sprints started adding up.

By the end, no one was talking. It was silent aside from Z barking orders to start and then calling out times as the clock expired.

Darko's teammates were furious with him. We had two other 6'9 players on that team that were both pretty tough dudes too. We'd find out later that there would be a fight back at the dorms with Darko after practice with some of his teammates who were so mad at him. But it worked.

Sure, we still had issues that season including starting the conference season 1–2 with our only win being in double overtime. Z had gotten away from trusting his patented match-up zone early on in our conference season before he had a come-to-Jesus moment and stuck with it the rest of the way.

After that double overtime win, we'd lose our next two games resulting in Z shouting "burn the boats!" He was implying we'd stick with the match-up zone no matter what happened. We'd go on to win 18 of our next 19 games before finally losing in the final four to the eventual national champion, South Plains.

You see, sometimes we need tough love in our lives when we'd least like to have it. I witnessed it first hand with a team that fought it tooth and nail for the first half of the season before we all saw the light—saw the good that could come from the structure and discipline that Z was putting in place. The structure and discipline that I would help him instill with this amazing group of guys.

I feel a bit like Darko back in 2007. I was ultra-talented, and I kn? but lacking discipline, lacking structure, and relying on talent to g by when there is so much more there that simply needs to be harnessed and then released.

That transformation has begun, and I can't wait to see the results. I have no doubt that the next year will yield the personal results that our team accomplished in that historic run at Seward County.

DAY 24

Circle of Life

Lesson Learned – We can want so badly for something to work. We can fight like hell, make the changes on our end, do everything we need and want on our side, but if both parties aren't working together and communicating effectively on what they're trying to accomplish then it won't matter for either side. Whatever it is will ultimately fail.

Lowest Low – Danielle says she's single. That's awkward.

Owen,

It's 10 p.m., which is late for me these days. I didn't take my melatonin yet as I have to catch up on some things both work-wise and personally including some journaling.

Today was a strange day. You and I started things off normally with breakfast and then off to your school around 9:30 a.m. I ran by the bank to clear some things up financially with the business. It was all pretty normal.

Here's where it's been a difficult balance for me, however. Danielle sent some texts last night talking about how she wanted to be with me,

135

and then some more texts this afternoon talking about how she wanted to run away or needed a vacation. Half serious and half joking, I think.

What makes it challenging for me is that I want to be there and comfort her. I even told her, "Let's book a trip with fully refundable tickets in a month, and see where this goes." She didn't think that was a good idea and ended that conversation immediately. She would have been right.

Things went deeper than that in that she also implied she was single. I think she meant she's not ready to commit to getting back together with me or telling people publicly that we are working on things. She mentioned she doesn't want to go through the ups and downs again.

I understand that. I don't think she meant single in that she is actively pursuing or even open to dating other people. But I haven't asked her that explicitly. Tomorrow I will.

I hope it goes well. I hope it's not the end of what we're trying to repair. But it feels like dramatic swings from time to time on my side, and that's hard on me right now. I know things are hard for her too.

There is going to be no easy way out of this shit, and I know that. I wish we could establish a plan for our repair, if one exists.

It may be unrealistic and impossible to establish a plan right now because we are both healing and don't know what this is yet. I don't know, but it all feels fucked up right now. Or the unknown feels fucked, I should say.

I think I want to be with her under the right circumstances and work with her on getting back together in a healthy space. But for us to be having sex regularly again and her staying the night but still saying she views herself as single was tough to hear and tough to take. I'll know more tomorrow.

She did give me a timeline of three months today. Maybe that's the timeline of us continuing what we are doing to move toward her feeling comfortable enough to begin to tell others about us again.

I think more than anything, with the events of the last couple days, I'm reminded that you can want something in life as bad as you want. You can work at it, whatever it is. You can change, do better, give good effort in the situation, and all those things. But if the other person isn't committed and isn't willing to work with you on making the changes then it's going to fail. It's a lost cause.

This situation reminds me of the best player I ever coached, Tony Smith. He is the most talented player I've ever coached. I don't say that lightly.

Tony was 6'5 and long. He could shoot the ball to three really well, had incredible court vision, and was super athletic. Tony could finish above the rim. Tony was also a point guard. That's a pretty incredible and unique set of skills for a PG.

I first saw Tony at an availables event after his senior year of high school. Available events are where players from high school are still trying to find a school late in the school year, usually in March or April. It's generally not good to still be available then. That usually means you aren't talented enough or you have some red flags, and so people don't want to have you on their team.

In Tony's case, he didn't graduate high school so he was going to have to go to junior college. It was just a matter of which one. I saw the talent immediately. I fell in love. I had to coach him. The fact that he didn't graduate high school didn't bother me at all. We'd figure it out.

The event was in North Carolina, the Greenville area where he was from. We talked after the camp, but he was hesitant to come back with me all the way to Kansas.

The Greenville area, East Carolina in general, has a unique dynamic to it. Family is huge there. There are some pretty rough areas, and no matter the talent level, a lot of players just stick around and go to school locally. Some don't go to school at all. Greenville just eats them up, and their careers end.

Tony was almost one of the latter. After that first sighting, he would sit out the next year. I didn't get him to Seward County until the second year I recruited him. He'd eventually come to Kansas, and we'd get him his GED. Tony had a killer first season for us—so good, in fact, that he was invited to the best junior college player summer camp in the country after his freshman season. Once invited to this camp, you are labeled a high-level Division I talent. You'll have high majors recruiting you your sophomore season. Tony did.

The list included Kansas, Kansas State, Florida, North Carolina, and about every other blue blood you can think of outside of Kentucky and Duke.

He was so good that Oklahoma State came to watch us play in Coffeyville (fucking Coffeyville again, I know), and Tony played so well that a high major, Big 12 school, offered him a full-ride scholarship after the game the first time they saw him play. That NEVER happens. He was that talented.

The one area that people would question him, coaches included, and the part of his game where he and I often didn't see eye to eye was his motor. That's how hard he played the game.

I was a 6'3 point guard with limited ability. I could shoot OK, pass really well, and was an above average athlete but nothing compared to Tony. I could always control how hard I played the game and how tough I played.

Everyone can control those two pieces of their game. To me, those pieces are not debatable. You should always play as hard as you can, and you should be tough.

Tony struggled with those pieces because of some deeper issues—personal issues I didn't understand at the time. I didn't see that then, and I didn't understand until it was too late.

Our relationship started to strain his sophomore season of junior college. Coach Z, the uber demanding coach I mentioned above, was hard on everyone. Most could take that, but some couldn't. Tony was OK with Coach Z.

The problem was I was always the good cop to Z's bad cop. I patted guys on the back. I told them he was crazy and to let go whatever he may have yelled at them for that day. But with Tony, I was just as demanding. I wanted him to do so well that he was being coached by two bad cops now.

We were both on him every day to play harder, to be tougher. He was getting worse not better.

By the middle of his sophomore season, he wasn't even starting anymore. A 5'10 local kid that was tough and very coachable was starting at the point guard position now. Tony was ten times better than he was. The kid would even tell you that to this day. Everyone knew it. But we were trying to motivate him. We were trying to light a spark.

Nothing worked. Tony quit with four games left in his sophomore season. All those high major schools would take their offers back. He wouldn't graduate junior college, which you have to do in order to go Division I if you don't qualify initially.

I was devastated. He and I didn't talk for years. It was too painful for both of us.

He'd go on to have an amazing Division II career, obviously. He recorded several triple doubles which are incredibly hard to record. He'd go on to play overseas for a couple years landing a couple NBA tryouts along the way.

I don't remember who reached back out first, him or me, probably him. But we reconnected and slowly started repairing our relationship. I even coached him with some of the mental training exercises I do with professional coaches and athletes. It really helped unlock some unconscious limiting beliefs he had, some of the dark places in his life mentally and emotionally.

We both felt better. Our relationship is great now. The only person in my life that I'm more proud of to this day would be you. That's saying a lot. He's done that much with his life.

Here's the heavy part of that, however. Most of the time in really difficult situations and relationships, we think we are giving our best. Both sides think they are trying their hardest, which means that a couple things have to happen in order for situations like these to succeed.

First, you have to be willing to admit that whatever it is you are doing isn't working and both sides have to change. Most relationships can't get past step one.

The relationship has to mean enough to you that you say, "I value this, the success of this relationship, more than my ego." I couldn't do that back then. Tony couldn't either.

It feels like Danielle and I are there too now. Her ego is wanting me to take accountability for everything, to apologize for everything, and to continue to do that moving forward, to do everything exactly the way she wants and needs me to do it. And maybe I should?

I can't do that, at least not yet. I also don't think I should because that doesn't feel healthy to me.

Second, you have to move on from the past. Whatever was done, let it go and focus on the present.

Understand what I'm saying here. Don't excuse negative behaviors. Don't let partners cheat or hit or anything to that degree. But we also have to have communication and empathy for things that have taken place in the past. Then if the two sides agree that they are willing to work on correcting them, they have to stop dwelling on events that have happened earlier on in the relationship.

This can happen a couple times, saying things are going to change and that things will be different. But then, ultimately, you have to draw a line in the sand and say, "stop." Either make the changes we are agreeing to, the changes that need to be made, or we need to move on from each other.

That happened with Tony and me. Both sides drew the line. Neither blinked, and he quit.

It feels like Danielle and I are getting close to drawing a line in the sand. I don't know who will draw it or why, but it feels like it's dangerously close to happening. I fear what that could mean for her, for me, and for us.

Time will tell.

DAY 25

An Evening on the Brink

"HAVE YOU EVER LOVED SOMEBODY, LOVED HER COMPLETELY,
BUT HAD TO END THE RELATIONSHIP FOR LIFE REASONS?"
—JOHN MAYER, MUSICIAN

Lesson Learned – It's much easier for me to see the value of the Sacred Pause—the space between a stimulus and a response—now that I'm sober. I've always been so smart, so naturally gifted, that I could just talk and bullshit my way through things even when I drank.

That wasn't the best version of me. That was a fake version—a version that usually led to poor results and poor conversations at least compared to my now sober standards. I much prefer this new version of the sacred pause—of listening empathically and of having a more genuine conversation.

Lowest Low – Today was the first day where I thought that the relationship with Danielle was in serious jeopardy. Before, when I was losing my shit in the first few days, I was irrational and emotional—a wreck and I knew that was on me. Today was different, and tonight felt different.

Owen,

141

Today was a wavy day. I was as low as I've been since week one, maybe even day three or four of week one.

It's hard to look back and reflect on all of that and compare emotions. All I can say is that I know I felt like shit at one point today and throughout most of the evening. We'll get to why in a minute.

Yesterday ended in a weird space. I can tell Danielle has some things on her mind, some heavier things. But she starts the day with an "I love you" text, and I respond with the same. It feels like the calm before a storm.

I think it's time for us to start having conversations on where things are headed, when, and perhaps most importantly how, so I shoot her a text and ask if she can come by to talk about everything.

Danielle says she can't but calls at 3 p.m. instead, and I dive right in. I start explaining earlier conversations I've had today with my therapist—what's fair for her, what's fair to me, and what's respectful for both.

Asking her to try and give dates or clarity on these things has her triggered. She reminds me that she doesn't know when she will be healed, if ever. According to her, it's manipulative to ask her to commit to getting back together with me in an aggressive tone.

Danielle has always been bad at saying really triggering and powerful words like that without much pause—words like manipulative. She does the same with other people. I don't like to use those kinds of words unless it's really extreme behavior especially toward my partner.

I think when we deal with people in general, it's important to try and release ego as much as we can, focus on behaviors and actions, and what are you actually trying to do. The talking part is surface level and always felt gossip-like to me whether it was with Danielle or even a former player for that matter.

If you make a mistake, don't tell me you're going to fix it. Start fixing it. The talking about it part to me, or to others, never served a purpose. It's probably why my circle was always small and tight, and I don't talk much to others about larger details.

Yes, I'm aware I say that as I write a book about a failed relationship and recovery from becoming too dependent on alcohol, but hopefully you get the point.

That has also become part of the challenge in repairing the relationship with those around Danielle and me, in my opinion. I don't tend to share our fights or use negative vocabulary when describing her behaviors. That never made sense to me.

If either of us really felt that way then we should end the relationship. If not, if you're just upset, don't say something to someone close to you that you'd regret when the relationship is repaired. People are quick to bitch about problems, but those same people are usually pretty slow to brag about the positive behavior of their partners.

But who am I to tell her how to feel or what words to use and vice versa? I do know that we can't walk back those words once we use them especially to family.

As we talk more, I communicate that I'm not asking her to commit but just to say if she's open to it and what that would look like. I remind her that she mentioned the three months of healing yesterday, but she says today that was a response she felt almost pressured into saying.

This is a good example of what I'm talking about. By asking her for a timeline on things since we are having sex already and moving back into relationship-type activities, I assume we are on that path. I think most people would. Yet when I ask that question, I am being manipulative in the relationship and forcing her to say and do things she doesn't want to do.

To me, it can't be both. Either we are moving forward with our activities, which is great! Or if the relationship and my behaviors make her feel this bad, this manipulated then we need to end it. I don't understand the confusion.

It's hard to imagine this conversation going much worse at this point, but then it does just that.

After she starts to raise her voice on some of these topics and tell me that maybe it's best for us if we go back to barely talking and seeing each other (fuck!), she then dives into a lot of the shit I'm already getting hammered with in my healing. Things I know I need to address in my past. This is hard for me. I have to be careful about how I respond to this for a number of reasons.

With my troubles with alcohol, I always had an excuse for my behaviors. This part I now see.

There were manipulative behaviors, straight bullshit.

Once you get sober, no one wants to hear any of your bullshit explanations. They want you to listen and shut the fuck up, rightfully so. So I sit there and take these truths about how my relationship with your mother needs to be repaired, how all my past relationships have all failed because of that one hanging over all of them.

I'm guessing she means over the past couple years since your mom and I divorced.

No shit.

I chime in that it actually goes back further than that to my parents' relationship and how bad that was for me to witness, how that was a sense of what I thought a normal relationship looked like. I don't try to explain all of this right now. I just sit there on the phone and listen getting emotional as I do so.

She dives deeper into me and my drinking and how it affected her and my relationship. I continue to listen.

I don't say that in a negative way. It's just the truth. It's important for her to get some of this shit off her chest. It's important for me to just listen. It's most important for her to hear me not make excuses or say shit aside from, "OK, I hear you. I'll work on it."

I'm crying now on the phone. She can tell.

"Are you OK?" she asked.

"No," I responded.

"Well can I do anything for you? Are you going to be OK?"

"Yes, I'll be ok." I say weakly.

"Are you sure? Was that too much."

"No."

One-word answers are all I can get out now without crying during my sentences. She can tell I'm hurt.

We go back and forth for another minute or two, and then I get off saying that's about all I can take for today. I'm going to go now.

Danielle asks if she can stop by after my yoga classes tonight, and I weakly respond with, "If you want."

I can't tell if it's out of pity or love or both. But I agree to let her stop by because I would like to see her. I just hate that I feel like this, and the direction our relationship is headed.

Or that it feels like it's headed in at this moment.

Everything feels like it's moving in slow motion.

The interaction now has me triggered. I would have drunk in the past, but instead I become intensely aware of emotions I haven't felt in a long time since I was with a past partner. Not your mother but someone I dated years ago.

It was a relationship with a girl back at Seward County. Her name is Ashley, we'll say.

Ashley was beautiful, Hispanic, and a really good athlete—a much better athlete than me, actually. She was an all-American in junior college twice, I think. Then she was a Division I player and finally a college basketball coach.

That's how we met there at Seward; she coached on the women's staff.

Ashley was going through a divorce. The circumstances of how we dated weren't the purest. We moved too soon, at times inappropriately even. I regret that part.

It was hard on her too as she was a good Catholic girl, came from a religious family, and divorce was a sign of failure not only in your relationship but in life.

My parents went through a nasty divorce, and so I could give a shit less about that part. I was more worried about if we would be able to make the relationship work with her being so fresh out of the separation and then divorce. Time would tell.

Ashley and I started dating, and it became increasingly difficult for her to get through the day. What started off as occasional heavy drinking turned into drinks on occasion during the middle of the day—a shot of whiskey at noon and maybe two on another day.

Neither of us would ever be drunk in the middle of the day, but we were now drinking to stop feeling. This is the first time I remember doing that in my life especially to not feel in the middle of the day.

I'm not sure why I would join her in doing it, to be honest. Even now, as I reflect back, it was like I was doing it to help her feel better not that I wanted to drink. I didn't.

But that would open a Pandora's box with regard to that type of behavior being OK. I wouldn't drink in the middle of the day except for a few times that year. And then not again for a decade or so after that, not until recently.

I remember feeling guilty as I did it then. Feeling like I was letting the team I was coaching down. Feeling like I was letting myself down, but that I was genuinely helping her feel better. And that, it would seem, was more important than anything else.

Even as I type that, I don't believe that to be true, but that behavior would reflect that when I was coaching back then—that her, our relationship, was more important than my career, than the team, than anything else in my life for that matter. It was a strange time.

We'd continue to date on and off for the next couple years. The last year of it was long distance. Ashley couldn't take the small junior college town talking about her or at least what she thought was gossiping about her and her divorce. So she moved back to Las Vegas where she was from.

After a year of a really challenging long distance relationship, I'd eventually asked her to move with me to Pittsburg State when I took the job there. We could both reset, and we could start anew.

She agreed. I was pumped. We even looked at places together. She came to visit me in Pittsburg, and she knew some of the coaches that were already there from her playing days. It was going to be great for us both.

We even went to Mexico together on a vacation with her brother and his wife and one of their friends. The trip was amazing and was one of the best trips of my life.

When I got back to Pittsburg after that, she started to get hesitant again. Her family didn't really know me as in her mother and father. And they weren't comfortable with her moving in with me because she was divorced, and we weren't engaged.

I told her I wasn't doing a long distance relationship for another year. She needed to move to Pittsburg, or I was done trying to make this work.

Ashley felt like she couldn't go against her family, her culture, and her religious beliefs. I felt like her family and her religion shouldn't be dictating her life especially if that's not what she really believed and if that's not what she really felt.

And I know she didn't feel that way. I know she didn't believe the things those around her were telling her to think and feel. But she felt like she had to do it.

So that was it. I told her I was done.

Two years of dating, of random day drinking to numb our pain, of drinking to get her through a divorce and into our new relationship—none of it worked.

It all fell apart, and it ended.

I think that's the point, the struggle with alcohol and what it does to your decision-making abilities. Initially, like with Danielle even, it makes things easier. The problem is it makes it easier to arrive at both good and bad decisions.

That happened with Ashley, and that's happening with Danielle.

Now that I'm sober, today is a reminder that some of these difficult emotions and thoughts that I'm having in my relationship with Danielle are similar to the ones that I had with Ashley. That scares me.

I don't think it should be this hard. Maybe I'm wrong.

I understand there will be difficult times. I understand there will be sacrifices. I understand that if any relationship is worth it to you, if the person means that much then you have to have those difficult times and conversations, work through them together, and come out better on the other end.

I don't know why, but I haven't felt that way with anyone yet—not Ashley back then, not your mother when things got really tough, and not with Danielle now.

That's really tough to write. I need to explore those emotions, that line of thinking. Is it me? Why haven't I felt that commitment, that level of sacrifice yet? I think the reason is, quite honestly, that I believe it shouldn't be that much work when the person is right for you.

If it's the person you want to be with, that you should be with, and that you know you can't be without then I don't think it feels like work. I think it just feels right, something that you both know needs to be done.

It's similar to the difference between doing something as a job versus doing something you love. When you're doing something you love professionally, it no longer feels like a job. The passion you feel and the commitment comes naturally. You want to go to work, and you want to keep improving on your passion.

There are difficult times within the profession, sure, but you don't waiver in your commitment to it because it feels like you were meant to be doing it. I have found that now in what I'm doing in my work with professional and college athletes—helping others awaken and be balanced mentally and physically. In helping them achieve total mental and physical well-being, I can tell this is what I'm meant to be doing, and I love it even on the challenging days.

I feel the same with you. The love, the commitment I have for you and helping you grow is almost unexplainable. I'm so grateful for you, for our love, and for what we have together as father and son. Sure there are challenging days there too, but I love you just the same.

Shouldn't our relationships with our partners be the same way? I think so, but I'm still looking to find that. I'm still searching for that love. I know it's out there, and I have a resounding belief that I'll find it with the right person. Who that is and when is still to be determined.

I thought it was Danielle. After these past few days and these past few conversations, I feel less and less sure of that.

DAY 26

Feel Good Friday

"IMPERFECTION IS BEAUTY, MADNESS IS GENIUS,
AND IT'S BETTER TO BE ABSOLUTELY RIDICULOUS
THAN ABSOLUTELY BORING."
—MARILYN MONROE, MODEL, ACTRESS

Lesson Learned – Feeling good, like most things in life, can often be about perspective. Millionaires can feel poor. I've witnessed people living on dirt floors in Costa Rica who were emotionally rich, filled with love and joy. We choose what we feel; we choose what we attract. I choose to feel happiness again. I choose love. I choose gratitude. I will attract those positive vibes, those positive emotions, those kinds of people into our lives.

Highest High – I'm starting to find self-love again—a grace with myself and the fact that I won't be perfect even in sobriety. It's nice to love myself again.

Owen,

It's interesting how things don't necessarily get easier as time moves on. It just flows differently. It becomes more about learning how to ride the ups and downs, the waves, and trying to not be too reactive in the process.

That doesn't mean we won't still feel emotions. It doesn't mean that things won't be difficult or even warrant strong emotions as I mentioned yesterday. I very much realize they will especially from her side. I did a ton of damage, did some really shitty and selfish things. I know I have reparations to make to the people I affected.

It's been interesting to find more self-love even in my mistakes in sobriety. That wasn't always the case. At first, I was harder on myself. How can you still make these mistakes when sober? Why are you still sore today when you're sober? Why do you feel hungover when you didn't drink last night?

What I realized was that my drinking would make it worse and that I needed to practice one of the most important pieces of mindfulness, of meditation. That's self-love, forgiveness, acceptance.

I'm also reminded of the discipline and the sacrifices I've made in the past few days, which then causes me to reflect on the discipline and sacrifices I made in my life. The newfound discipline I have in not drinking takes me back to some of the proudest moments of my life.

The sporting highlights I mentioned in the days above. From the age of five, I've done incredible things mentally and physically as an athlete. I've made mistakes, sure, felt pain, and failed over and over again. But then, every once in a while, you get a real high. It's like a drug. And you get sucked right back in.

I had those experiences as a coach too.

Taking my team to a final four, being a part of record-setting seasons, I had some really high highs. I don't think any of them compare to the first time I coached at Allen Fieldhouse playing against what would be a final four team down two points in the second half and having the time of my life coaching against a hall of fame coach and a couple future NBA players.

I'll never forget pulling up in our team bus the first time we played the Jayhawks. I didn't follow Kansas that closely. I didn't realize the weight of the program, the history, and the fandom we'd soon be encountering.

We were an average Division II basketball team and the students were already lined up outside the ticket office waiting to get in. Two hours they'd wait just to see their Jayhawks play against what was supposed to be an otherwise normal Division II opponent.

The students didn't care. They wanted to experience Allen Fieldhouse and the Jayhawks. They wanted that high too.

KU was supposed to be good the year we played them. How good was still to be determined. It just so happened they would wind up in the Final Four as this Jayhawk team would get hot late in the season anchored by the 7'0 Jeff Withey in the middle, an NBA talent in Thomas Robinson, and solid guard play from Tyshawn Taylor among others.

The result of the game wasn't as important as the experience for me and for our guys. We were like kids in a candy store. Eyes wide open playing against future millionaires on the court.

Shaking hands with the coaching staff before the game you can't help but think about the fact that you are shaking hands with a future Hall of Fame coach in Bill Self. That was cool too.

The part that most people don't realize is that once those guys step off the court, the coaches and the players, they're just people. Sure, some of them are cool, smooth talkers just as personable and talented off the court as they are on it.

But a majority of athletes, coaches, even celebrities are surprisingly normal once you get to know them. I don't mean that as a negative. I mean that to make you feel better.

Those emotions that we all feel—the difficult times, the awkwardness that in our personal lives, in our relationships, at work or at school—they all feel it too.

That's the piece that is often misunderstood when we see these athletes and coaches on TV. We somehow think they are immune to what we think and feel. We think they're immune to emotions, dark thoughts, failure just because we see them on ESPN or because they have money, fame, and athleticism.

They get sick. People in their family die, suffer from addiction, or struggle with their mental health. What happens to us all happens to them too.

Unfortunately for them with power, with fame, with athleticism, there is also this cloak of invisibility we expect them to have from feeling anxiety, negative emotions, from failing.

I think that's what makes it even harder for athletes and coaches to accept failure. I think that's what makes our relationships tougher especially when they fail. We, as athletes and coaches, are taught that we MUST succeed. In every avenue of our life. We can't fail. We don't fail. And that's simply not true.

We fail every day. If you don't fail, you're not getting better.

When you lift weights the way your muscles get bigger is by lifting until you fail and then your muscles recover and you get bigger as a result.

With our meditation practice we don't start out meditating for an hour. We start with a minute. Even then your mind may jump all over the place. What most would then consider failing is actually not a failure at all. It's a shift in awareness; it's your first rep. That's a good thing.

The point being it's OK to feel these emotions, the good and the bad. The key becomes moving on from them. Leaving the emotions and thoughts behind. Not dwelling on them or firing what's known as the second arrow. Letting one bad play, or experience, or thought snowball into several other bad plays, several other bad thoughts, days worth of bad experiences.

Understand good and bad things happen to us all. That's life.

Label the thoughts, feel them in your body then move off from them. These thoughts don't control you; the experiences don't control you. If and when you can master this, and you can, you in turn won't need to lean on any substances to help you in controlling your emotions like I did.

And that's one of the most powerful experiences I can provide you in your life just like the Jayhawks did for me that day.

DAY 27

Fireworks

Lesson Learned – What I want versus what I need and what is healthy with life, with love, and with alcohol. I see I need to step back and reevaluate that.

Lowest Low – The biggest challenges seem to continue to be how to navigate the space in what was an old, unhealthy relationship and the new one. The path I used to go down versus how to navigate the new space, the new road, the new journey you and I are on now as a family and if Danielle comes with us on that journey.

Owen,

Another emotional day today. Shocking, I know. You saw Danielle for the first time in over a month.

Danielle then decided to come by later in the evening, which makes both you and me extremely happy and grateful. We decide to shoot off fireworks that Danielle has had since the Fourth of July, which I think is the last time you saw her. That's almost 8 weeks ago.

A shadow hangs over the night for me, however. A cloud may be a better way of describing it with the fireworks we shoot off tonight.

There are all kinds of smoke bombs, sparklers, and snappers that are toddler friendly and you both have a blast. I think you like the bright colors of the smoke bombs best. You haven't quite figured out sparklers yet. They are still intimidating for you to wave around.

Age can affect a lot of things in life such as our experiences with fireworks, our experiences in sports, falling in and out of love. Almost all the most impactful experiences of our lives are affected by age—some more than others.

I'm drawn to things that make me feel alive. I'm starting to see that now.

Take alcohol, for example. It turned me into someone different when I drank it. I became more social and more outgoing. It was a different version of me—one that I mistakenly thought was a better version of me.

But that lightness, that positive effect, was starting to fade quickly toward the end.

Someone who had been a fun, outgoing, energetic person with a few drinks had now become someone that needed several to feel anything. I now needed five or six drinks to feel the effects of what only one or two would have done before and what one or two would do for most people.

I've always been naturally reserved, calm, and collected—difficult to rattle as a person and as an athlete. That was great on the court, but it frustrated my partners.

The fact that I kept to myself and was a reserved person when I wasn't coaching also made me attracted to women like your mother and Danielle—beautiful, young women that liked to drink and go out. I found myself naturally drawn to women that were fun, outgoing, social, and entertaining.

Almost all the women that I seriously dated fit into this mold. I see that now too.

I don't mean this as a negative, either. This is what a lot of men look for in their partners—fun, outgoing, and beautiful women that like late nights and are incredibly passionate in a variety of ways. It was like another drug for me. Women like your mom, Danielle and others that made me feel more intensely and more deeply than I was accustomed to. It was another way, like alcohol, to make me feel alive.

I also see, perhaps ironically, that's not what I'm looking for in a partner now. That version of me is gone, and that Ryan no longer exists.

My therapist recently had me do an exercise where I listed the characteristics of my ideal partner. It wouldn't include many of these traits anymore. Beauty? Yes, of course. I define beauty differently now though.

That isn't meant to knock your mom, or Danielle, or anyone that is an outgoing, emotional, social, and loud person. As I mentioned, I see now that almost everyone I hung around with, be it male friends or female friends, fit this description because they were providing me with what I thought I was missing in my life. I thought they were the perfect complement.

The part I didn't understand was that the relationship worked better when alcohol was involved. They worked just OK when it wasn't. Therefore, they never lasted.

We didn't know each other without it. None of my friends or partners knew me—the raw me and the vulnerable me. No one did.

I didn't.

Alcohol would ramp up my energy allowing me to match theirs. I'd become more emotional like them—more outgoing too.

We became closer to each other almost meeting in the middle of what our true behaviors were, how we communicated. We became aligned with alcohol.

But sober when stressors presented themselves, I see now why things would become so toxic. They would become more emotional and more outgoing. I didn't like that.

I'd become more reserved—my true behaviors. I would talk less. I would avoid confrontation. Or I'd just go drink to solve the problem. Sometimes, we'd go drink together so that the problem would go away.

It wouldn't, of course. Alcohol just kicks the can down the road. It never makes it go away and only numbs your pain until you are ready to face whatever the problem may be. That or the problem becomes so pressing you have to face it, usually drunk. Not surprisingly, when you try and solve problems from your relationships to important professional decisions with a cloud hanging over you, it doesn't go well.

Or it's not what you or your partner, your business, and your team actually needs. When drugs or alcohol are involved, the line of thinking becomes, "Whatever, fuck it, I don't care anymore. That's fine."

I see that now. That in these relationships, we were just delaying decisions that needed to be made by drinking. We were masking our true problems, the differences that existed, and the problems that wouldn't go away until we faced them. But we had to do that sober.

Your mom and I never did that. Danielle and I tried. It was too late for us too, at least it appears so. She's still so guarded. Even in moments of joy like tonight, it's like both of us are waiting for the proverbial shoe to drop.

Don't get me wrong. Tonight was fun. I am glad to have her back in our lives. I hope things work out. But I can't help but feel these larger issues that I see now will continue to hang over the relationship until one of us addresses them. By all appearances that will have to be me. It's just a matter of when.

The same was true of your mother and my relationship. While we didn't fight early on in our relationship, hardly at all for the first six months, a big reason why was the alcohol consumption and constant distraction of me being a college coach. We were always happy as a result—carefree, lighthearted. She was my light in what was a terrible and dark professional season.

Your mom was only 21 when we got engaged. She was 22 when we got married, still 22 when she got pregnant. She was 23 when she had you.

I think time is relative as I've mentioned before. But we were still figuring each other out at a deeper level. We should have spent more time together learning about each other, our interests, our desires, our thoughts, and our passions—the things that really make a relationship work.

We should have focused on how we could help each other grow, improve each other's confidence and raise our self-confidence, self-awareness, and self-love.

I think, like a major part of this book has shown, things unfold the way they did for a reason. Neither she nor I regret anything that happened or that we did. You are the best thing to happen to either of us. You fill our lives with so much gratitude, joy, and love.

For that, we will both be forever thankful.

It's also true that your mom and I, and even you, are still figuring things out and how that will look for all of us as we move forward. Your mom is headed back to school looking for a new profession in the medical field. My business continues to grow and blossom.

I think back to those early days with your mother, the early days of us dating. She was 21 when we met, by all of like three weeks. She was young, outgoing, social, and liked to party. She checked all the boxes of whom I was drawn to in a partner.

To me, that's the big takeaway from today. When we look for partners we need to find people that compliment us, that make us better. I was always looking for a partner (or alcohol) to make me happy not to compliment my already existing self-love. My self-love didn't exist. Therefore, an ideal partner also did not exist.

Alcohol, women—I tried to fill those voids in my heart and soul with all kinds of temporary fixes, temporary solutions. That didn't work.

You have to love yourself first then a healthy partner can complement and take that love to another level. When you find that hold on to it, work on it. That love is something worth fighting for.

DAY 28

28 Days Later

"THERE'S NO POINT IN GETTING TOO WORRIED ABOUT THINGS, BECAUSE LIFE IS TOO SHORT."
—DOLORES O'RIORDAN, LEAD VOCALIST OF CRANBERRIES

Lesson Learned – Just like the zombie apocalypse ending, I feel like the zombie form of who I used to be is starting to come undone. The antidote has been found. The cure? No alcohol. Easy enough, right?

Highest High – Learning to meditate peacefully under the most intense circumstances imaginable.

Owen,

Today was a great day filled with lots of love, joy, emotions, and happiness.

You and I head to Target one last time before we leave for your birthday festivities in Springfield. It will be awesome to see your aunt Megan and her new baby, the rest of her family, and my mom and dad. I'm guessing there may be an awkward moment or two without drinking.

Megan and her husband, Logan, and I usually tie one on once the babies go to sleep whenever we are in the same city together. At least that's what we always used to do, but the more I step back from these situations the more I realize that most of these common drinking experiences were as a result of me wanting to drink not others. It's amazing how the frequency has almost died completely with the people in and around my life now that I don't drink.

I know a part of that is the fact they want to be respectful in my sobriety, but I also realize that a big part of it was that I was always wanting to drink, not necessarily get drunk, but drink for sure.

It wasn't that way in high school, but when I got to college and then into coaching it was usually my idea to drink. I always said yes when someone asked me to go out, and I always said yes to another drink. There's probably some deep-seeded desire to be loved or accepted or successful at drinking.

Toward the end, I actually drank less in quantity but more often. It would start sooner. Sometimes I would start in the mornings and then when I got drunk, I'd get really drunk. As I've mentioned before, I was drinking now to numb and to not feel, and that's when I knew it was time to stop.

Your mom had tried to get me to stop a couple times in the end of our relationship. It was difficult to stop then for lots of reasons.

She and I drank way more when we met than when she was asking me to stop. I didn't understand that part. Why are you saying I have a problem now when we drank way more than this earlier in our relationship?

The answer was simple, you. And I was drinking way less but still too much for her. It wasn't affecting my parenting. I was always around, a good father to you, never neglecting responsibilities personally or professionally.

After emotions became too intense in our relationship for a number of reasons, including alcohol, it was no longer healthy for us to be together. More importantly, it wasn't healthy for you.

I wasn't going to let her and my problems affect you and how we parented you. Our relationship had become too toxic because of faults on both sides of the relationship, and so it was time for me to leave. I did.

A couple months later, as we were finalizing paperwork on the divorce, your mom had asked me to wait to file the paperwork until after a meditation retreat I was going on for seven days in California. She wanted me to wait and see if there was a chance we could make it work. I knew there wasn't, but what was another week to me? I agreed to wait until I got back.

As I was walking into a seven-day meditation retreat, mostly silent, where I would be meditating around eight hours a day, I got a call from your mother. She had filed the paperwork.

She knew I was going to file regardless, and that I was going to end the marriage. Your mom wanted me to wait so she could get custody of you for the month it would take to process the paperwork. Over that period, I'd only get to see you one day a week. By far and away that was the least amount of time I had ever spent with you. That was really hard to process. It was cold.

I'm now walking up this long and winding road to a monastery to attend a seven-day meditation retreat having all these thoughts and emotions running through my mind. I had to sit, mostly in silence, with all these thoughts and emotions. That was the best possible thing that could have happened to me.

I read, I wrote, and I meditated. Most importantly, I started the journey of self-love. I tried to find forgiveness and empathy for your mom.

That journey took a little longer than seven days.

But it's happened. Your mom and I are in a good place now. We're in a place of mutual respect and love with a common interest in wanting amazing opportunities for you and your life. This includes a desire as co-parents to put you in the best possible situation we can so you can succeed mentally, emotionally, and physically in life.

As I try to do that for myself 28 days after my last drink of alcohol, I can't help but see the parallels there in our past relationship with it being destroyed and now rebuilt.

And then in how my life has unfolded.

The relationship with your mother was like a shooting star; it burned brightly and quickly.

My relationship with alcohol lasted a long time; it was a slow burn. It felt more like a zombie apocalypse—biting one piece of my life, one relationship after another until everything, everyone, and everywhere was infected.

When I saw there were only a few places left to go and that the world would soon be ending, I had to find the antidote.

For me, that's not drinking.

DAY 29

A New Normal

Lesson Learned – Relapse in this new world is very common, and I see why. It is a razor thin line between knowing too much and thinking you have this thing fixed and then falling right back down on hard times.

That's the delicate balance of what I've experienced and also the hesitation I have in publishing this book. It helped me to look into the physical and mental effects of alcohol, to know why I felt and acted the way I did. That becomes a challenge for most in their sobriety—thinking they can solve the problem logically with discipline. You can't.

Lowest Low – What does an allergy or disease of alcohol mean? I don't get that. I dove into that discussion and more today with a friend.

Owen,

One day away from 30 days, which is pretty cool to think about. I talked about that in a meeting I went to today.

Time is still relative. I feel that. This month felt like it flew by; this also may have been the longest month of my life.

162

The first week especially crawled by. I remember days one through four felt like an eternity. 24 hours seemed like a year. Now I enjoy being sober.

One of the things I realized along the way is that you spend about six to eight hours a day in some kind of alcoholic fog either spending your hours at night getting more and more intoxicated or spending several hours in the morning recovering.

Even on the days I was disciplined and only had a couple beers and a shot I was not sharp those nights. I had that drinking fog in the morning.

It's been so nice to be sharp and alert for all of my day again. It's helped me to remember so much more, to stay sharp for so much longer, and be more productive.

I told your mom about my sobriety today. It's the first time we discussed at depth that I realize now I can't drink anymore and that my long bouts with sobriety were good but were misleading in that it's obvious now that I can't drink responsibly for long periods of time.

Alcohol feels like it ends with me being in the elevator that leads down. It's not a matter of whether it will lead me down. It's just a matter of how far.

I hadn't planned on talking to your mom about it, but she was supportive and is relieved that I am getting help. I'm sure she feels validated to some degree too as she had problems with my drinking later in our relationship.

I reflect on the difficult times of our relationship, of me drinking. I'm not sure if one caused the other or if, most likely, they made each other worse.

One of us would usually get triggered, cause the other one to get triggered, and then a situation would escalate. Your mom would get mad, say mean things, and I'd drink because I hated to argue. I'd remove myself from the situation. She'd become more upset as a result. Some variation of that was a summary of most of our fights.

That happened on repeat for about two straight years until one day I left. Needless to say, there was a lot of healing needed for both of us and our relationship. Luckily, it never affected us or our ability to be good parents for you.

Some of my reading today discusses alcohol as an allergy. How then does it take 20 years for it to set with some people? Why does it take eight years for others?

In asking some of these questions to those around the recovery world, I get some good but surface-level answers to the question.

I ask why some males and females can start drinking at the same time, but a woman becomes an addict much more quickly. Apparently, females are more likely to ramp up their drinking more quickly than men. They also usually do so later in life than men.

The biggest discrepancy I have is that how can I have drank for 20 plus years and just now be in recovery? If I am allergic to it, why haven't I always been? I don't agree with this line of thinking. I think I drank too much probably through some combination of depression and lack of success in a number of areas of my life. As a result, I chose to drink. Then it grabbed hold of me, and I couldn't break loose. I needed someone to shake the shit out of me, metaphorically.

Another question is: If I have a disease, why didn't this disease attack me sooner?

I learn the science behind why these things happen. Details they cover widely in *This Naked Mind*. But the AA folks don't like to discuss this because most people begin to think they can solve it on their own. They think they can fix it. They can't.

It did help me to read the details on it all. I don't know if I'd have remained sober without it.

Most of those around me continue to hammer reading the AA books. I went to a couple meetings today, and it's been a long day. After meeting first with a sponsor before the group meeting, I'm at this random church for almost three hours. That made for a long day of healing, of reading, and of thinking.

It ended up being a long day and then a late night—one that involved lots of studying and lots of research. That sounds and feels familiar. While this particular night was studying alcohol and the recovery process, it reminds me of how a long day of coaching felt. I haven't felt this exhausted, mentally and physically, since my coaching days.

You practice plan. You watch film on future opponents, or on your past games in order to prepare for the next one. Those 16-hour days where you are coaching, scouting, planning, and watching film. I used to miss those days when I first got out of coaching.

I miss those days very rarely now although the initial transition was very difficult.

We don't talk about transitions enough as we have already discussed in the book. But let's circle back to that. Why don't we talk about transitions when we are losing a piece of ourselves, of our perceived identity? Why isn't that a bigger deal?

I was a smart, successful, driven, and well-off 30-something white male, and it was hard as hell for me. I can't even begin to imagine what that transition is like for others that aren't as fortunate as me.

I couldn't even watch basketball (college or professional) for a year after I got out of coaching. It was too raw.

It was like seeing your ex all the time on TV, seeing her doing well and still flourishing without you. That shit hurt to feel and to see.

And that pain still existed with the school I left failing miserably that next season just like I knew would happen. I had warned the head coach and athletic director, but they couldn't see it or didn't want to.

So I chose to leave. I chose to move on.

The game moved on from me too. It always moves on. It's like water in that regard. It's going to keep flowing. You can ride the current, ride the waves for a bit. But eventually it's going to go through you or around you.

If you still don't move, it will destroy you.

For example, think of all the people out there that actually caused the game to ripple and changed the game. Think of the number of athletes that, when they left, the game struggled for a minute without them. We could take any sport, but let's focus on basketball for this example.

Bird and Magic changed the game and then Isiah had a run. Jordan reigned for a decade plus and then Iverson tried, unsuccessfully. Shaq and Kobe, Duncan, Dirk, and Nash all had moments. Along came LeBron and his generation with D-Wade and then Love and Kyrie. Curry, Thompson, and Harden stretched the game forever. Kahwi and Giannas seem poised to be next with Luka on the horizon.

There's been like 20 dudes in my lifetime that changed the game of basketball.

What about the rest of us? The game has moved on with barely a ripple.

That's life too.

30 days in and my life moves on. Danielle and I are fading with my emotions and feelings for her doing the same.

What felt like a person I knew I couldn't live without now feels a person that is better off without me. It's now a relationship that can't and won't work—just like I saw with basketball in the end.

I love you, but it's time to move on. It's not you; it's me.

That's how I felt with basketball then. That's how I feel with Danielle now.

DAY 30

Navigating a Storm

"BUT MAN IS NOT MADE FOR DEFEAT.
A MAN CAN BE DESTROYED, BUT NOT DEFEATED."
—ERNEST HEMINGWAY, WRITER

Lesson Learned – A storm blew through yesterday, emotionally. A day filled with ups and downs has turned into a much better, calmer space today.

I'm being hammered over the head right now with practicing patience and caution, feeling raw emotions and pain. Caution and pain aren't always negative signs. Caution signs help us to not crash, physically and emotionally. Sometimes, we feel pain to keep us safe too.

Highest High – 30 days sober. It feels great. People have come and gone over these 30 days, really important people in my life. And I've been pushed in ways mentally and physically like I wouldn't have thought possible, but I made it. We made it.

Owen,

Perhaps ironically, I have you when 30 days hit, but how do we celebrate? What the hell does a celebration for something like this even entail?

As I wind down the first 30 days of being sober, I can't help but zoom out on the last month, on what I've learned and what I see now.

Danielle and Susan, such integral pieces of the initial recovery are now out of my life. Susan is out completely, and Danielle is rapidly heading that way as we continue to make each other worse not better.

The pain I feel internally, emotionally, and physically still exists. It occurs way less often, but it's still there. If anything, it's more raw, more vulnerable, and more accessible. But I like that. I actually enjoy that. It gives me a sort of clarity I've never experienced before.

That's what is difficult about growth, I think. Things are so uncomfortable initially that we never reach the actual change stage of the process. We get out of our comfort zone for a little bit—maybe a few days, maybe a couple weeks, and then we revert back.

It doesn't last.

I see that now and how that cycle has happened for me in a variety of ways and a number of times in my life. The stretching out of your comfort zone, coming close to that growth occurring, then reverting right back.

I didn't realize it until I started writing this book, and until I reflected back on my career as an athlete and coach. But the desire to avoid pain and not feel raw experiences started in college. I was already drinking to not experience deep emotions and to avoid being raw and exposed when tragic things happened in my life. That started with the loss of a teammate when I was just 20 years old.

When I was playing, I'd get bumps and bruises along the way. Let's use a severe ankle sprain as an example. I'd take six or seven Ibuprofen to not feel anything. It helped me perform and I enjoyed that Pink Floyd's *I have become comfortably numb* type of feeling. When I played, I felt like it allowed me to play better without feeling anything. I doubt it did these things.

Then it moved into my life as a coach. Win the game, drink until you are comfortably numb to celebrate. Lose the game? Drink until you're comfortably numb to not feel as sad.

Whatever it is, don't feel. Never feel too sad or too happy. That's the safest route to take to be happy. That way you can't get hurt. Sure, you won't be as happy, but you won't be as sad either.

Right?

Wrong.

It took me 39 years and exactly 8 months (I checked) to figure this out.

It took the highs and lows of a wildly successful athletic career where my uniform was retired at one school and most likely will be retired at a second school.

It took multiple successful and then failed relationships including a marriage to your mother.

It took the birth of you and the loss of several friends and family members.

It took a 12-year coaching career with record-setting success at every single stop along the way but ending with a dud at the last stop.

It took me starting a business, and it almost failing several times, but me persisting as an entrepreneur for what is now an extremely successful athlete meditation and mental fitness app.

It took me almost dying a few times, first at the age of 12 (I was sober for that one!), then again this year.

It took Danielle supporting me through that stop in ICU where I almost died, then us losing a child that was a few weeks old, and then us eventually losing each other's love.

It took lots and lots of alcohol. I tried to drink it all, but I couldn't do it. It wasn't for a lack of trying.

Then one day, which I'll always remember for as long as I live, I decided that was enough. I was tired of fighting that fight. Alcohol and I needed to break up. We were in an abusive relationship.

I wanted to feel again. I wanted to feel everything. I needed to feel everything.

If my business was going to succeed and if I was going to live the life I was preaching, I needed to do it sober. I needed to live the life I was telling others to live.

How could I tell others to practice mindfulness, to meditate, and to practice yoga if I wasn't living a life that way? I couldn't. And honestly, I wanted to start to feel again.

I wanted to be raw, exposed, and vulnerable.

I wanted to feel intensely. I wanted to love deeply.

I wanted to have my relationships be healthy and consistent—full of love, support, and have way less unnecessary highs and lows.

Physically, if there was pain, I want to feel it. I want to breathe through it. I want to use the power of meditation, the peace of mindfulness, and the mind-body connection of yoga.

Emotionally, if it's difficult, I want to figure out why. Let's work through it. Let's establish if the emotions are something worth continuing to struggle through, to suffer through.

Mentally, I want to be in an incredible place through learning, reading, and growing. I want to take my thoughts, my emotions, and what I have learned on this journey and share it with the world allowing them to learn from my experiences, from my thoughts.

That's what I was meant to do, not be a really good drunk.

And that's what I will do for you, for me, for my future partner, for my family, and for my business. I'll be sober so that I can live my life's purpose. What that will look like is still to be determined.

But I have zero doubt that now my impact on the world of athletics will end up being incredibly powerful. It will help coaches, athletes, and even those that struggle with some powerful imbalance with a drink, a drug, or another destructive habit to look at it and approach that problem in a new way. To see that potential problem in a different light. A healthier light.

This Naked Mind talks about how once you start drinking, you are like an insect that flies into a meat-eating pitcher plant. It's not a matter of if you get eaten but rather a matter of how quickly you decide to descend.

My descent was slow for the first few years of drinking then escalated rapidly and stayed there for 20 years or so. Then the last two while isolated here in Kansas City, personally professionally, went to another level.

Last year, I finally got eaten whole. The habits were there, the powerful drug alcohol was slowly doing its work, and once the stars aligned this past year with all that's gone on, it was too late to get out.

I used to say to the basketball teams I coached that once something became noticeably a problem on the court, when it became a problem during a game, that means it had been a problem for a while.

My drinking had become a problem. I was just doing other things well enough to cover it up.

Talent does this often for sports teams. You can be so talented that it doesn't matter how effectively you do something.

The same is true in life. I was talented enough to fake it for years when alcohol had become a problem for me. I was charming, funny, successful, and good-looking—all the things that made it easier for me to fake happiness, love, success, gratitude, and selflessness and to fake the things that really matter.

Alcohol also escalated the negative behaviors. I lacked patience, empathy, and kindness. I forgot things I would normally remember. I began to care less and less about things that would have normally been red flags for me personally and professionally.

The alcohol numbed and erased it all, slowly and cunningly, in a way that takes decades to accomplish. It takes even longer to notice while you're caught in the middle of the long-lasting storm that is addiction of any kind.

Now that storm has destroyed most of what I had in life, but it didn't wipe me out. If anything, it cleared out all the bullshit from my life.

I was lucky enough that my physical and emotional bottoming weren't so bad that I lost everything. For that I am extremely grateful. Most importantly, I didn't lose you. I was smart enough, loved you enough, and could still fight it enough that I was always a great father around you.

Today is Day 30, and I owe a big piece of me making it this far to you. You were there for me in so many powerful ways, emotionally. I'll be forever thankful to you and so many people that got me through this life-changing month with their support.

I'm grateful to you and for you. I love you. I'm insanely proud of you as you just turned four. I'm insanely proud of me too, the person I now am, and the person I will become—the mindful father I will be for you, the mindful brother and son I will be for my family, and the mindful leader I will be for the world of athletics and for MindSport.

DAY 60

Castaway

Lesson Learned – Life isn't a movie. There aren't many fairy tale endings. No matter how badly we may think we want something or want something to work, most of the time, it doesn't work out exactly like that. It doesn't work out like we have envisioned.

That's not a bad thing. In fact, it's a beautiful thing.

Highest High – It's weird to say this, but there's a peace with my relationship ending. I know it won't be over like the snap of a finger. It will be like most of this book—a ripple that slowly fades. But I accept that, and I'm ready for that.

Owen,

60 days have come and gone since that fateful night I last drank. I'm still sober. Things are going really well. MindSport is taking off in some incredible ways. Physically, I'm back to my playing weight when I was in college. I'm as strong as I've ever been.

Mentally, I'm clear, feel lucid, and my writing and the content I am now producing is at such a higher level now it's incredible to experience.

The best part is seeing others enjoy the content, seeing what I produce help others, like this book will do.

Last week, I stumbled on the movie *Castaway* while I was unwinding on a lazy Sunday night. I couldn't help but notice all the parallels—how that movie wove in and out of what felt like my recovery.

The part that resonated the most? The ending.

The first time or two I saw it, I thought the ending was so unrealistic. It actually frustrated me.

The plot being Tom Hanks's character is stuck on a desert island for four years (four years!) with only a couple UPS packages, a volleyball, and a Monopoly timepiece that has his fiancée's picture in it. After going through all of these terrible experiences like having to knock his own tooth out, rubbing his hands raw to learn how to create fire, and fishing with a spear made from a tree, he miraculously escapes.

After a few days on the open water, he is spotted by a boat. He's saved.

Amazing! Hanks and his fiancée he left behind will now be reunited. Their love being the only thing that kept him alive these past few years. It has to be that way, right?

Hanks goes to visit his fiancée, Helen Hunt, at her house. He realizes she has a family, a husband now, and a child. Things have changed. She had to move on.

After a quick conversation, Hanks finds out she still loves him. She runs out to him in the pouring rain, romantically kissing him, asking what they will do next.

Hanks says she needs to go home. They'll both need to go their separate ways. What the fuck?

I was furious at first. They should be together. That's not how things work! That's not how life works!

The truth of the matter is, more often than not, that's exactly how life works. There are not these romantic endings we are hoping for, that we think we need.

As humans, we teach lessons and we learn lessons. We face great times and we face difficult times. We land a dream job and then get fired.

There is no good, and there is no bad; it's just our journey in life. Each of those events teaches us a lesson.

The same is true in love. We find someone in our lives we swear we can't live without. We dance, we laugh, we kiss, we love, and we have sex; it's incredible.

Then we break up.

We realize we've grown apart, or that we're not meant to be with each other. That it will be too tough, or someone gets sober, or the family becomes too much of an issue or some combination of a thousand things that can happen and the relationship ends. And that's OK. Life goes on.

It feels heavy as hell at first. We think we'll never find love like that again. That one was too unique, too perfect, the sex was too good, or they understand you in a way that no one else will. That's not true either.

The truth is that person isn't meant for you at that time. Something is happening in the world, a ripple, that's causing that relationship to no longer work. It's causing you two to drift away from each other in a way that's best for you both.

We can still love the other person, really love them, but it can also be true that the relationship no longer works. No one has done anything wrong; both sides are trying as hard as they can. It's just not working. Life must go on.

Both sides are trying to talk, to communicate effectively, and to empathize and understand the other person's perspective, but they don't agree. It wasn't meant to be, and that's OK.

That happens in life too. Castaway endings happen in love every day. Well, minus the plane crashing, volleyball loving, and expert fishing lead character.

The other parallel? Alcohol was my Wilson, Hanks's volleyball friend.

Like Hanks with Wilson, I felt that alcohol was extremely important to me. I knew that it wasn't helping me succeed at all, but I felt like it had to be around in my day-to-day life. I felt that almost love for alcohol like Hanks had for Wilson.

Hanks loses Wilson during his escape and is devastated. That very much felt like my first couple days sober—emotional, a wreck, and full of emotion over something that wasn't real—something that was an illusion, like Wilson.

I tried and tried to function successfully with alcohol being an integral part of my life. I tried to save it, save it being a part of my life. I couldn't. I had to let it go.

When Wilson floats away, Hanks surrenders; there is an acceptance that occurs on his journey. Whatever will be for him now will be. He's let go. He's surrendered and no longer worries about what will happen. Literally and figuratively, Hanks actually releases his paddles from his life raft.

He has accepted this is now his path in life.

The same happened for me once I let alcohol go, and once I surrendered. After time, a comfort washed over me. I know now, for the first time in my life, that I am on the right path.

As an athlete and even as a coach, I always felt that I was destined for something different. Not necessarily better, well yeah, it was always something better. I felt as though I wasn't accomplishing what I was meant to accomplish in life.

I felt weighed down. I felt heavy. Now I am light.

The last piece of the puzzle when Hanks gets back and finds his girl is with another guy. He is figuring out his next steps in life, his journey. I think what he realizes more than anything is that starts with a self-love and that his girl can't provide that for him. That his love must come from within.

I'm doing the same thing now. I'm practicing that self-love, that self-compassion that I told my therapist I couldn't do in my first week. I didn't even know where to begin.

A journey that started two months ago with me not even being able to love myself has evolved into a relationship with my mind and my soul that I am now incredibly proud of for so many reasons.

Everything in life starts with self-love. That's our foun
most important piece in life. You have to feel that, and you
that deep down in your heart.

If we don't know, truly know in our soul that we deserve good things to happen then they most likely won't. That's the law of attraction.

Life may not play out like a movie, and it may not go exactly how we see it in our minds, but we will attract what we believe. And the path will start to uncover itself that will lead us where we were meant to be.

My advice to you, Owen, is to surrender to your journey in life.

You can't control it, and it won't be perfect. All we can do is be present for it.

There will be many ups and downs and a million ripples in your life.

You can't worry about those ups and downs, the ripples.

Focus on self-love and on your love for others. Handle your life with not only that powerful love, but compassion, empathy, kindness, mindfulness, passion, and an incredible joy that covers you like a warm blanket.

Do that, and you'll end up exactly where you were meant to be.

You're on the right path.

DAY 90

The Vision Unfolds

"WHEN GOD DECIDES IT'S TIME, I GUESS HE'LL COME FOR US"
—DIEGO MARADONA, SOCCER PLAYER

Lesson Learned – A funeral of a former player takes me to Wichita where a flood of memories come rushing back. The death of Marky Nolen, the celebration of his life, and the drive to and back symbolizes not only a death for him but what feels like a death of an older and toxic version of myself.

Lowest Low – A flood of emotions on a drive up and back to the funeral of a former player of mine feels almost like a death and rebirth for me too. One version of me dies, and another is born.

Owen,

90 days of sobriety. 39 years and now 10 months of living summed up in a day.

A funeral of a former player takes me to Wichita, where a flood of memories come rushing back. Marky Nolen was his name. He leaves behind four children and a beautiful fiancée. He'll never hold his kids again and never get to kiss, hold, or make love to his fiancée again. That makes me feel raw, sad, and vulnerable.

All the most beautiful experiences in life are gone for Marky, yet the world marches on. It's a cold world in that regard. The three-hour drive to Wichita gives me plenty of time to think about that. That and more.

Marky was the toughest player I ever coached. Marky was this ball of energy you felt any time he walked into a room. He was the only player I coached twice, and although we lost touch a few years after I coached him, his life and then death is very symbolic of where I am at in my life, and where I was headed without this awakening.

When I got the news about Marky a little over a week ago, I would have normally been so raw and upset that I would have drunk, and I would have wanted to numb the pain. Instead, I wrote a heartfelt post and put it out on social media.

It goes viral. Within a week, it has over 600 shares and raises over $7,000 for his family, for his children.

Days like that, and days like these are where I start to see the beauty of sobriety and what it does for not only me and my path in life but how that starts to ripple out and affect others in my wake.

If I'm drunk, I don't write that post. If I'm not sober it's not as heartfelt and not as raw, which is what makes the post more authentic. That sobriety, that emotion, and that vulnerability is what people relate to because that's how people feel. They want to share that. They want to be able to share what they are thinking and feeling even if it's not them that wrote it.

As I'm driving up, I have time to reflect on not only that but all these places along the highways of middle Kansas where I spent a majority of my coaching life. Hotels where I stayed with a team I was coaching, hotels where I stayed while I was on recruiting trips, and hotels I stayed at to meet up with past partners.

All the good and bad emotions, sensations, and thoughts come flooding back.

I'd probably be drinking right now on the drive if I wasn't sober. I wouldn't want to go into the funeral sober, so I'd have bought a beer or two for the drive or stop in Wichita to get a shot or two before I headed over to the church.

That thought enters my mind as well—what the old Ryan would have done. It would not have been the mindful decision; it would not have been the one that felt more, thought more, and loved more.

I like this version better.

I arrive at Marky's funeral, and the air outside the church is filled with marijuana smoke. There are some people drinking in their cars. That used to be me.

I think about that too. Would I have normally come up the night before to drink with friends and family? Would I have stayed tonight after the funeral so I could drink with the friends and the family after the funeral?

This is another part of drinking I don't miss. How it controls you, your time, and your decision-making.

Instead, I head in sober and find a spot in the corner. I listen to everyone paying their respects.

The pastor doesn't really know Marky. He's doing his best, but I can tell his surface-level view of the situation is that Marky got caught up in the streets. Wichita, Kansas has some rough pockets in it filled with violence, shootings, and stabbings. They're all getting more and more common in some of the rougher areas.

I see it differently.

What I see is a bright star in Marky, one that burned insanely bright and one that couldn't sustain that brightness. He burned off energy too quickly, and he lived his life too intensely.

Even when he was confronted by his alleged killer with a gun, reports said that Marky said, "You ain't gonna do nothing."

Think about the courage, and some would say stupidity, it would take to dare someone to shoot you. The killer obliged by shooting him six times in the chest.

Marky was so tough that he asked his friend to take him to the hospital. He thought he'd survive.

Marky's life was relatable to me. I mean that not because of our lifestyles or our backgrounds. Those could not be more different. Instead, I mean that because of where my life was headed and how intensely I was burning the candle on both ends, working long days of half-assed work.

Alcohol affected my performance at the start of the day, and then I would spend most nights counting down the hours until I drank again that night. Sometimes a little, most nights quite a bit, and some nights a lot.

I was daring alcohol to shoot me.

Luckily, I walked away before alcohol could pull the trigger.

That was the difference in our lives among other things. But I'm reminded of this fact as I listen to this pastor talking to those in attendance of making better decisions in their lives.

The pastor brings up a good point. One that I think he should have expanded on.

What if Marky's life, what if his ripple, saves the life of one or two of his boys that would have got caught up in the streets? What if his children swear off drugs, alcohol, and violence all because their dad got murdered in front of them at a youth football game? It could happen.

I feel that going on in my life now 90 days after my last drink.

I feel like all of these experiences in my life were meant to be shared with the masses to help athletes, coaches, and those struggling with similar battles. I mentioned most of that on Day 30 of this book. I'm reminded of it with Marky and his funeral.

As the funeral finishes up I head home and have that long three-hour drive home.

This time, thankfully, I'm sober.

I passed several liquor stores on the way out of town. The old Ryan would have stopped and got something for the long drive back. I also dropped a larger check off to the funeral home that took care of Marky and his services. It was the last of the funds from the fundraiser that took place as a result of my heartfelt post.

Once I hop on the highway, the memories come back again, not fading, almost like they are being released. It feels like a slow surrender to the new life I've found.

The best way I can describe it would be a sort of energy leaving my body, floating away because it can't find peace within me anymore.

That dark wolf I talked about at the beginning of this book has become frustrated with me. It wants me to give in. I won't. I can't. Not today.

I realize this journey, not only the drive I'm on currently but also the longer journey of life; will be filled with challenges like Marky's funeral.

There will be new partners that I fall in and out of love with, new relationships that will be difficult initially with my sobriety. A new girl will appear in my life, (not a Danielle, not a Laura) someone who is different from both of them and all of my partners. That's good.

I'm different now as I said in Day 27. What attracted me then to women doesn't attract me now. I don't attract that now either. That's not a good or bad thing. It's growth; it's change.

I attained that awareness of love in my sobriety. I've learned what a healthy partnership looks and should feel like.

I'm grateful for that.

There will be challenges with my business in terms of finding the right partnerships, helping athletes see the benefits of mindfulness, of meditation, mental fitness and of sport-specific yoga.

Athlete meditation, mindfulness, and yoga are still ahead of its time. It's catching up though. I'm not going anywhere.

I've learned patience in my sobriety. I've learned a healthy determination.

I'm grateful for that.

There will even be challenges with us. Our relationship won't be perfect, but it will be perfect for us. I'm excited that I am in a much better, healthier space for you to take on the challenges that we will face together. Physically, mentally, and emotionally we will be prepared to take on those challenges.

I've learned to be better prepared for the unknown in my sobriety. I've learned acceptance, and I've learned nonjudgment. I've learned how to be a better father.

I am grateful for that.

I am grateful for you.

That feels like an appropriate way to end not only today but this journey. Ending it with a newfound clarity, a newfound self-love, and a newfound acceptance.

I'm also fully aware that the days, months, and years ahead will be filled with ups and downs for you, for me, and for everyone reading this book.

But just remember that all of those ripples that take place in our lives lead us down the path that we were supposed to be on.

Don't worry about where you have been. Don't worry about where you will go. Stay present. I know I will.

One breath, one drop, and one ripple at a time.

Conclusion

Professionally things have really picked up. MindSport, my other child, has taken off.

We have partnered with some heavy hitters in the sports world, professional athletes that are aligned with us in the mental fitness, athlete meditation, and yoga space. We are starting to really gain traction or what's known as hockey stick growth in the entrepreneurial world.

MindSport now offers sport-specific series for all these professional athletes that in turn helps out their followers or other athletes in their respective sports. We're starting to change their world and make the sports world a healthier space.

I'm incredibly proud and grateful for that.

When people talk about our vision, my vision, it's about causing a shift in how sports is perceived and how success is defined for these athletes. We are going to do that. We are doing that.

All of the experiences I went through in life, the ones you read about in this book, led me to exactly where I was meant to be, leading this company into a space that will revolutionize the way athletes train, coaches coach, and how we balance training.

What used to be 90, 95, 99 percent physical will now start to shift into significant percentages of mental training.

Who knows what the correct balance will end up being? Well, the answer is no one knows. But the promise is in the fact that we are now shining light onto it and helping athletes and coaches to not feel and struggle like I did.

I'm incredibly proud and grateful for that too.

I know the app and the books I have written will help accelerate these shifts. We are starting to have the necessary conversations. We are starting to integrate mental training, mindfulness, athlete meditation, and sport-specific yoga.

We're no longer waiting until athletes are broken to fix them. We're being proactive.

We still have a long way to go.

Honestly, we're probably a decade away from where it needs to be in creating the right balance. But MindSport and I will continue to stay ahead of that curve. We will get there.

There was a similar resistance to lifting weights in the early '90s that there is now to mindfulness and athlete meditation. Weightlifting was frowned upon by basketball players until they saw Jordan and Pippen lifting on game days as the Bulls were busy winning NBA championships.

My high school coach wouldn't let me lift weights in high school during the season and that was the late '90s. It takes a while for these ripples to reach the distant waters.

Nutrition was the next wave. High major NCAA schools started bringing on nutritionists in the 2000s. Colleges of all levels started bringing them on board in the early 2010s.

Sports psychology came next. In 2021, NBA teams will require a sports psychologist on staff. That's a step, but it's not the answer. Sports psychology is a resource, but like AA was not for me in my recovery. The mind works differently for different people. That form of treatment doesn't work as well for every athlete.

What then does the future of sport look like? How can we offer multiple forms of mental well-being to athletes of all levels?

How do we balance their mental well-being with the fact that we do need to push them out of their comfort zones mentally and physically in order to achieve greatness? How do we really make a difference for our athletes?

There's a lot to unpack there, and it would probably require another book. But let's take the time to at least answer what we can do for athletes right now, and how we can make things more affordable and accessible to the masses.

The answer is simple. Tap into the money and power around the higher level of sports then modify the levels of convenience and comfort around them for athletes. Do this at the highest levels, and the implementation will then trickle down to the other levels like it always does.

When we as a society worry less about donating money so that we can have our name on a seat in a gym and instead donate $10,000 so the team can hire a personal mental fitness coach, we are starting to move in the right direction.

The problem with a proposal is you have to have a forward-thinking booster club and a forward-thinking administrator, a forward-thinking owner of an NBA team and a forward-thinking coach and GM. The right combinations must be in place, and they must join each other on the right path.

Both sides must value mental well-being over temporary satisfaction of a new weight rack, a new piece of equipment, or the possibility of spending it on a recruit that they may or may not even sign.

Like anything in life, it's about sacrifice, and it's about balance. How many professional teams down to the NCAA levels are willing to take the piece of the financial pie and invest it in more meaningful areas—areas that can't be seen? Areas that can only be felt at the deepest and most meaningful levels? This is why I mentioned it will take years to play out.

MindSport, for example, is starting to have professional team owners in the region reach out about meditation pods and program implementation in their new facilities. These facilities are spaces where athletes can practice visualization, breath work, and deal with anxiety and stress among other powerful pieces.

Teams need to start looking for mental trainers on site, at all times, like we do with athletic trainers. They don't have to be sports psychologists, but they do need to offer mental training, mindfulness, and yoga in some form.

Athletes need to have access to these resources just as they would a gym, a weight room, or a team dining hall.

Once we start to bridge that gap then the tide starts to shift back into the athlete's favor in being able to balance their emotions, the negative and positive thoughts in a way that becomes healthy for them and their families. The need for unhealthy habits starts to fade. Total athlete well-being takes a front seat again.

What's now seen as the dark side of athletics is instead brought to a positive and healthier light.

We begin to realize it is in fact not darkness at all. It's normal to feel these positive and negative thoughts and emotions.

The dark side would be to ignore our thoughts, our feelings, and our emotions as they continue to control us and our lives. When we do this, we turn to alcohol, drugs, and destructive habits so that we don't feel them and don't have to process them.

This is similar to what alcohol did for me when I was looking to solve my thoughts of inadequacy as an athlete, a coach, and then an entrepreneur. It wasn't healthy. It was fucked up, but it's what I did to cope for 20 years.

I know now that it's OK to be sad, frustrated, and angry. What's not OK is to stay there. These skills, these teachings through mindfulness, meditation, and athlete yoga can be learned, can be taught, and will help heal.

As a society, especially in athletics, we need to accept all of this and the sooner the better. Once we do, more and more athletes will rely less on alcohol, drugs, sex, violence, or whatever the dark side is for them.

One drop, one inhale, or one bad habit at a time will start to fade away. They won't be gone completely, but they won't be as controlling as they were earlier.

Awareness levels are now shifted, and players and coaches are now equipped to take on the challenges that I took on in this book without the bottoming out that I had to go through in order to get there.

My bottom was terrible. I don't wish it on anyone, but I was lucky in that I survived mine. Others aren't so lucky.

Every quote that you see above, every quote to start each day is from someone who is either in recovery or died from their habits, from their addictions.

An intentional list that includes the most talented and famous athletes, writers, musicians, and actors our world has seen over the past 100 plus years. This further illustrates that the darkness does in fact touch us all. Lots of athletes, writers, musicians, and actors have had One Last Drop.

Let's all do our part to make sure those last drops are in recovery and not in death.

Acknowledgements

Time for some love...

Let's start with my parents, my mom and dad. Two totally different types of relationships, but both help in their own unique way.

My dad has been an extremely calming influence for me the past few years. His compound, as he calls it, is where I go when I need to get away for a few days. It's where I went the first weekend I was sober.

He's been an incredible influence and has shown tremendous support and grace to me the past few years as I've transitioned a few times in life not really knowing what I was doing or where the path I was on was taking me.

He keeps supporting me on this path, a path I've fallen off of several times. That's a big reason why my relationship with Owen is so important to me along with the examples that I provide to him, mostly with my actions.

My dad saw greatness in me in times when I didn't see it. He wouldn't let me settle. For that, I'll always be thankful, grateful to him. He changed my world so that I could help change the life of Owen and so many others along the way.

My mother was one of my biggest supporters as an athlete and continues to extend that support in my adult life. I appreciate and love her for that.

Love for my sisters, all three of them. Megs and Nikki, my actual sisters. Then Greta, my cousin, who is like a sister to us all.

Nikki was incredible in the beginning of my recovery. I'm not trying to romanticize the help she provided, but I don't know what I would have done without her that first week. I was in a terrible space, and she helped me dig my way out.

I need to thank Danielle for so many reasons or more accurately Hannah. She saved my life twice. I'll be forever thankful for that. My life and this book are both tributes to her and her incredible impact on my life.

While I wish things would have ended differently for us, I see now that they ended the way they did so that we both could remain healthy. The irony of that is not lost on me.

Our path was intense and impactful, and it was also meant to end with us apart.

Susan or Sue. Thanks for being there especially early on. I'll never forget that savasana outside the first time I practiced yoga when I became sober. I cried in corpse pose for ten solid minutes with her hand on my heart.

I wish things would have ended differently for us too, but I've learned to not question why things end the way they do. That energy and flow of the unconscious and conscious mind always takes us where we are supposed to be.

There's a new love for Owen's mom, Laura. A love and respect now that we are successfully co-parenting and doing what's best for Owen. It's a healthy friendship I appreciate. I know Owen does too.

This Naked Mind was imperative in my recovery more so than any program or book I read along the way. It was exactly what my mind needed. Just like I mentioned athletes connecting with mental training and well-being differently, my mind connected with *This Naked Mind* so well that it allowed me to shut off the desire for alcohol in a way that I never thought possible.

Thank you to the author, Annie Grace, for that. Your words were exactly what I needed to hear in a way that I needed to hear them.

She'll probably be mad I'm doing this but I need to recognize Patricia Wooster, my book coach. If you guys would have seen the original jumbled mess this started out as, you'd laugh, or run away in fear, or both.

She took a raw, exposed, vulnerable, and incoherent manuscript and not only helped me turn it into something that made sense but also helped me to carve it into the extremely impactful (I hope!) book you just read.

There's love for the Conscious Athlete Guide and app, and the athlete community as a whole. It's nice to be at peace with the athletic world again. I did not feel that way for a few years.

I'm even coaching again. I started coaching Owen and his four-year-old and five-year-old team. The circle of life that my dad started with me 35 years ago is complete.

I'm excited for the opportunity and excited to see the smile on Owen's face. I can't wait to see the happiness and excitement that he'll feel at practices, the joy and sadness he'll feel when games start up, and he wins or loses.

It will be fun to take in as a dad, and as his coach, as his athletic career starts witnessing the highs, the lows, and the ripples of his life. It will all be beautiful one drop at a time.

I just hope we don't play the Giants any time soon.

Thank You

Thank You For Reading My Book!

I really appreciate all of your feedback, and I love hearing what you have to say.

I need your input to make the next version of this book and my future books even better.

Please leave me a helpful review on Amazon letting me know what you thought of the book.

Thank you so much!
Ryan Stock

Made in United States
Orlando, FL
03 June 2023